WITHDRAWN

TWAYNE'S WORLD LEADERS SERIES

EDITORS OF THIS VOLUME

Arthur W. Brown

Baruch College, The City University

of New York

and

Thomas W. Knight

Adelphi University

Lincoln Steffens

Lincoln Steffens

LINCOLN STEFFENS

Russell M. Horton

Twayne Publishers, Inc. :: New York

Acknowledgments

I would like to thank my wife, Sharon Spencer Horton, and my friends Professor Russel B. Nye and Professor W. Cameron Meyers, for their advice and patience.

The passages from *The Letters of Lincoln Steffens* edited by Ella Winter and Granville Hicks and from the Introductory Memorandum by Carl Sandburg are copyright, 1938, by Harcourt Brace Jovanovich, Inc. and reprinted with their permission; copyright renewed, 1966, by Ella Winter, Granville Hicks, and Carl Sandburg.

The passages from *The Autobiography of Lincoln Steffens* are copyright, 1931, by Harcourt Brace Jovanovich, Inc. and are reprinted with their permission; copyright renewed, 1959 by Peter Steffens.

The passages from *An Not to Yield: An Autobiography* by Ella Winter are copyright, 1936, and are reprinted with the permission of Harcourt Brace Jovanovich, Inc.

The passages from *A Victorian in the Modern World* by Hutchins Hapgood, copyright, 1939, are reprinted with the permission of the Hutchins Hapgood Estate, Winchester, New Hampshire.

The passages from *Movers and Shakers* by Mabel Dodge, copyright, 1936, are reprinted with the permission of Curtis Brown, Ltd., New York.

Contents

About the Author

Russell M. Horton earned his Ph.D. in English: American Studies at Michigan State University. He has taught American literature and composition at both the high school and college levels, and has also taught English as a Foreign Language. He and his wife Sharon, also a teacher, currently live in Tokyo, Japan, where they are employed as teachers by Time/Life Educational Systems.

Chronology

1911	Josephine Bontecou Steffens dies. Visits family in California and makes brief European trip. Moves to Greenwich Village, and becomes editor of *New York Globe*. Goes to Los Angeles to report on McNamara case.
1914	Visits Europe. First visit to Mexico.
1915	Second visit to Mexico.
1917	First visit to Russia.
1919	Goes to Paris to report on Peace Conference. Bullitt Mission to Russia. Meets Ella Winter.
1920	Lectures on Russian Revolution across America. Moves to Europe, centered in Paris.
1924	Marries Ella Winter. Moves to San Remo, Italy. Son, Pete Stanley Steffens, born, November 21.
1925	Moves to Alassio, Italy.
1926	*Moses in Red* published.
1927	Returns to United States; buys home in Carmel, California.
1930	Last visit to Europe.
1931	*The Autobiography of Lincoln Steffens* published.
1933	Attack of coronary thrombosis on lecture tour in Chicago.
1936	*Lincoln Steffens Speaking* published. Dies, August 6, at Carmel, California; buried in family plot in San Francisco.

CHAPTER 1

A Constant Liberal

JOSEPH Lincoln Steffens was born on April 6, 1866, in San Francisco, California. The Civil War had been over only one year; and business, which was to symbolize the twentieth century, was starting its meteoric rise. His father, also named Joseph, was educated as a merchant in Chicago and crossed the frontier in 1862. In San Francisco he met and married Elizabeth Symes, who had recently come around the cape from New Jersey in search of a husband. Her success led to one son and three daughters.

Her husband's success, in business, led to Sacramento in 1870, and there most of young Lincoln Steffens's memories began. His childhood was free and easy, as he retold it years later in his *Autobiography,* and it provided him with numerous lessons about this world and its inhabitants. More than most people, Steffens would always draw particular pleasure from reminiscences of his youth.

Near the end of his high school years he was enrolled in a military academy, where he was to be cured of several bad traits typical of the Tom Sawyer era. After graduation he spent a year with a private tutor preparing to retake the entrance exams for the University of California at Berkeley. After finally entering, he earned a baccalaureate in history, claiming a position near the bottom of his class.

His desire to learn, however, had been kindled. Turning down an offer from his father to establish him in business, he traced the path of earlier American thinkers to Berlin, where he announced he was seeking a doctorate in philosophy, minoring in art history and economics. But his interests were unsettled, and he journeyed from Berlin to Heidelberg to Munich to Leipzig to Paris and finally to London, studying

11

first philosophy, then psychology, pursuing always art, music, theater, and the various pleasures of student life in Europe. He was in the proper frame of mind to profit from both formal studies and extensive European travel, and his first European odyssey freed him forever of the dangerous provincialisms that would block the critical perception of numerous other observers of modern American society.

In 1892 he returned to New York, secretly married to the former Miss Josephine Bontecou, an American student he had met in Leipzig. Thinking it time his son make his own way in the world, Steffens's father discontinued his son's allowance, not knowing about the new Mrs. Steffens. Young Steffens had planned to pursue a literary life, but necessity forced him to go to work.

Eventually he obtained employment as a reporter for the *New York Post*. Working a variety of beats, including Wall Street and the police station, he soon earned a reputation as an able reporter, generally allying himself with the reform elements of New York City. Newspaper work heightened his academically acquired perception. In 1897 he accepted a job offer, becoming the city editor of a troubled New York paper, the *Commercial Advertiser*. Collecting an assortment of young and talented writers, he transformed the journal into a literary haven for creative journalists, quickly giving the venture success and himself an enhanced reputation.

Newspaper work gave Steffens an insider's view of American society. On Wall Street he profited from a chance to analyze America's most sacred institution, business. Police reporting, on the other hand, revealed to him the underside of American life. He soon observed that the top and bottom of society were not really too far apart, and were closely connected by influence and graft. With new friends like reporter Jacob Riis and Police Commissioner Theodore Roosevelt, Steffens became a leader of what would soon be known as the reform movement.

In early 1894 Johann Friedrich Kruderwolf, a German student Steffens had befriended in Europe, died, naming the young journalist executor and major recipient of his estate. At twenty-eight, Steffens received assets totaling over ten thousand dollars, a sizable amount in 1894. When he returned to New York after settling the estate, Steffens invested it, using the knowledge of Wall Street he had gained as a reporter. The money served a far more significant function than assuring comfort. As Steffens recalled, he "slowly, surely, easily made enough money to make me free for life, as my friend Johann Friedrich Kruderwolf willed, free even of Wall Street." For the rest of his life Steffens never felt the necessity to compromise his integrity or honesty for the sake of security. " 'Money is not money,' " his friend Kruderwolf had told him, " 'it is liberty.' "[1]

Back in New York, Steffens's reputation continued to grow, along with his exhaustion from the increasing burdens of the *Commercial Advertiser.* Finally, in 1901, the same year an assassin's bullet felled McKinley and moved Roosevelt and the reform movement into the White House, Steffens accepted a position as the managing editor of *McClure's,* a successful new popular magazine. With this move his readership shifted from New York to the entire nation. While it had been gaining steadily over the previous ten years, in 1901 the reformist impulse suddenly became a national movement, and *McClure's* and Steffens were at the heart of it.

Steffens soon discovered that he did not have the patience for an office job. He left New York in pursuit of stories. Exposure of civil corruption, he observed, had been the source of great success for local newspapers. Reasoning that "some news stories . . . ran so long and meant so much that the newspaper readers lost track of them," he decided that "a monthly could come along, tell the whole, completed story all over again, and bring out the meaning of it all with comment."[2] This extension of news-oriented articles from newspapers to magazines was but one of several innovations that transformed the genteel magazine industry into a vital organ of social democracy and reform, leading eventually to magazines such as *Time* and *Newsweek* today. The first application of this idea was an article titled "Tweed Days in St. Louis" that appeared in *McClure's* in October 1902. Originally written solely by a St. Louis writer named Claude Wetmore, it had hedged in naming specific people and instances of corruption, a result of local pressure on a local author. Adding his name as coauthor to relieve Wetmore of blame, Steffens edited the article, adding the damaging information. He also decided that any further exposures would have to be written by him alone. Thus Steffens earned the distinction of being the first of that group of reporters later dubbed the "muckrakers." His next article, on Minneapolis, appeared with two other exposés, one by Ida Tarbell and the other by Ray Stannard Baker, in the January 1903 *McClure's,* establishing those three writers and *McClure's* as leaders in the publicity arm of the Progressive movement.

During the next decade Steffens was central among reformist journalists, basing a majority of his work on corruption in government and aiding the men fighting it. From his muckraking three volumes of selected articles were published: *The Shame of the Cities* (1904), *The Struggle for Self-Government* (1906), and *The Upbuilders* (1909). His national reputation grew at a rapid rate, and with it his influence increased.

Steffens became a man to be reckoned with: a powerful friend and a dangerous enemy. Men from all levels of public life turned to him for political advice and journalistic aid in their efforts to reform politics. Few men in the Progressive movement did not correspond with him; mayors Tom Johnson of Cleveland and "Golden Rule" Jones of Toledo, and editor Fremont Older of San Francisco, at the local level; Joseph W. Folk of Missouri and Robert La Follette of Wisconsin at the state level; and Theodore Roosevelt at the national level—to name but a few—all valued him as a man with a keen sense both of what the middle class felt and of how to implement reform.

Steffens remained with *McClure's* until 1906, when he and a group of other writers, mostly from *McClure's* and including Ida Tarbell, Ray Stannard Baker, Finley Peter Dunn, and

John Phillips, purchased the *American Magazine.* Steffens soon concluded that his financial interest in that venture might cause him to temper his reporting from fear of losing on his investment, and so sold his interest within a year. In the next few years he wrote several free-lance stories, a series of syndicated newspaper articles on the national government, and became a member of the editorial board of *Everybody's Magazine,* for which he produced a series entitled "It: An Exposition of the Sovereign Political Power of Organized Business."

During his first few years as a muckraker Steffens coined a term which has become an idiom of the American language. Speaking of the interrelation and interdependence of local, state, and federal governments with business, crime, and corruption, he established the label "the System." In one sense at least he spent the rest of his life trying to understand, and possibly reform, the sociological phenomenon he had, at least in name, discovered.

Politically, he moved to the left. As his knowledge of American politics increased, his belief deepened in the necessity of extensive and basic social changes far more radical than those sought by most Progressives. He came to see himself as far more than a mere disseminator of information; in 1908 he wrote to his sister, "I'm playing a long, patient game, but before I die, I believe I can help to bring about an essential change in the American mind."[3]

In late 1908 he accepted an offer from a Boston merchant and Progressive, E.A. Filene, to observe Boston and direct its liberal reconstruction. He started with high hopes of applying all he had learned. He spent a year digging deeper into civic government than he had ever dug before. Where his other investigations had been for articles, this one was planned to lead to two books, one on what was wrong and another on how to reform it. And, better yet, it was an active reform experiment with Steffens at the center. But the project came at the wrong time; the city was not ready for all that the liberal journalist thought necessary. The two books were never published; the city was never reformed.

His failure in Boston acted as a catalyst on Steffens's growing disenchantment with the Progressive movement. His close
contact with businessmen there hastened his growing impa-
tience with their self-righteous attitude; "the facts and the
meanings of [Boston]," he later wrote, "were so common; I
had reported the like so often that my mind or my stomach
revolted at the repetition."[4] He could not stand the unconscious hypocrisy of the reformers who were, he felt, in part
responsible for the corruption they sought to reform. And so
he changed his tactics—he would teach them to be honest with
themselves, rather than to be outwardly moral. He would convince them that they were guilty of all that they condemned,
not to reform them, but rather to eliminate their self-illusion.
For example, Steffens suggested to President Eliot of Harvard
that he be allowed to give a course to Harvard students, showing them how they were guilty of all the sins of government
that they sought to eliminate. When President Eliot asked if
his intent was to cure them from aiding corruption he replied,
"Oh, no. . . . All I want to do is to make it impossible for them
to be crooks and not know it. Intelligence is what I am aiming
at, not honesty. . . . What we need is integrity, intellectual
honesty."[5]

In 1911 Steffens's wife died, soon followed by his parents,
leaving him without home ties, disenchanted with the Progressive movement, and without a cause. He spent the next few
years wandering into various liberal social and political causes.
From his Connecticut home he moved into the intellectually
stimulating culture of pre–World War I New York's Greenwich Village, where he mixed with the radical youth of the
times, usually associated with the salon of the avant-garde
socialite Mabel Dodge. He started a habit of commuting to
Europe, rekindling his interests in the culture he had known
in his student days.

In late 1911 he became interested in the growing conflict
between labor and management. When two laborers, the
McNamara brothers, bombed the offices of the *Los Angeles
Times,* Steffens saw the situation as an opportunity to apply a

new theory of social reform. Leaving his newfound position of editorial consultant to *Everybody's Magazine,* he went to Los Angeles, where he attempted to convince the principals on both sides to apply the golden rule and to use the incident as an example of the futility of violence and revenge. Convinced that a proper start could and would alter the typical method of handling labor-management relations, he persuaded the McNamaras (and their lawyer, Clarence Darrow) that they should admit guilt if the management side agreed not to send them to jail. With the positive motives this charitable attitude would establish, Steffens felt certain that he could achieve an example-setting peaceful resolution to a labor-management dispute. When the court bowed to public pressure to go back on the bargain and jail the laborers, after they had fulfilled their half of the deal, Steffens felt even more convinced of the weakness and wrongness of "the System."

His earlier trips to Europe and his disgust with the outcome of the McNamara case made returning to Europe attractive, especially since his reputation in America had been seriously weakened by the publicity concerning the McNamara trial. With a vague intention of muckraking the capitals of the tradition-bound—and thus more intricately corrupt—old world, he started wandering. "All that I did," he wrote, "was to move about for years, a few months at a time, making what I told myself was a preliminary survey, such as I used to make when I first went to an American State or city, to see what the conditions were, in general, and where to dig for particulars."[6]

In America Steffens's reputation with the comparatively moderate popular magazine audience had been hurt by his association with the radical McNamara case. His lack of popularity with the public was reflected by a decline of popularity with editors. Since he was financially secure, he felt no desire to recapture public approval, although he missed the power he had once had. But he was moving in circles farther and farther removed from the middle-class norm; and his reputation, though later regained, would never be as broadly based or as influential as it had once been.

Soon after the McNamara case he reestablished a relationship with a California woman to whom he had been engaged prior to his first marriage. Although she had married and remained legally tied to her husband, she and Steffens renewed their affair. She accompanied him to Europe occasionally, and she provided him with companionship, affection, and the censure of his sisters.

In New York and Europe, Steffens's circle of friends changed dramatically from politicians and reformers to artists and authors. A few of the more liberal Progressives moved into the lively aura of radicalism with him, but most steered clear. Judge Ben Lindsey, the famed "children's judge" of Denver, and Senator Robert La Follette, men whose political careers Steffens had bolstered considerably, remained his friends for years; but even the liberal La Follette eventually parted philosophical paths from his old friend. The majority, the conservative and moderate element, gradually but surely moved into his background. The Socialists of England, the Communists and "intellectuals" of Greenwich Village, and the artists of Europe—mostly men a generation younger than him—became the society influencing and influenced by the retired muckraker.

Meanwhile, events in Europe moved steadily toward war. Unmotivated by the possibilities of reporting the coming conflict, and certain that "the inevitable war would bring on the inevitable revolution," he wanted rather to be prepared to interpret what the revolution meant.[7] Leaving the battles for other reporters, he returned to America, where he could study a small-scale revolution in progress in the United States' southern neighbor, Mexico.

In Mexico Steffens observed a people who had, as much as possible, thrown off "the System" that oppressed their individual freedoms. While their attempts at creating a new, socialistic government were amateurish, they impressed the increasingly radical journalist by their sincerity and their degree of success. Choosing one side in the conflict, that of the revolutionary Carranza, Steffens became as much an intimate of the revolutionaries as any American could.

He gained a reputation as a radical in Mexico from his magazine articles in favor of the revolutionary government and against American imperialism, and from his suggestions to the Mexicans on how they could write a constitution to make Mexico more resistant to corruption and foreign exploitation. This activity made him popular with revolutionaries, but it made him even more unpopular at home. However, through his friends in both the Mexican and American governments, Steffens found himself in a good position to work as a liaison for Mexico with the United States, since he knew the major politicians, the motivations, and the objectives on both sides. While it is impossible to measure the degree to which his involvement is responsible, it is safe to say that his assistance in the sensitive and volatile relations of the two countries played a part in averting a Mexican-American conflict in the years immediately preceding the United States' entry into World War I.

But the Mexican Revolution was merely a foreshadowing of bigger, more radical events. In 1917 Steffens was given the opportunity to travel to Russia to observe its recent revolution and assess the changes it had brought about. In the company of Charles R. Crane, a Chicago manufacturer and long-time friend of radical movements, and William G. Shepherd, a war correspondent for the United Press, Steffens embarked across the blockaded waters of the Northern Atlantic for Norway, and from there across the Russian frontier to Petrograd.

He arrived in time to see a revolution far more extensive and radical than the one he had seen in Mexico. The revolution in Russia, he wrote to his sister, "is a real one. . . . It is not over yet. There are intense issues to be fought out and the fight is on. . . . We are not seeing Russia alone."[8] Free of any specific duties, Steffens used his reputation and his connections among radicals to get as close as possible to the leadership of the revolutionary government. Here, at last, was something that was effectively destroying "the System" he so disliked.

More than anything within the new government bureaucracy, Steffens was impressed by what he believed to be the massive democracy of the freed Russian people. One of his stories, "Midnight in Russia," written soon after the visit, reported that after the revolution the people, *en masse*, " 'began to govern at once, naturally; they didn't, they don't know just how to take hold, or where; they don't know just what to do. But they took over, and they feel, each one of those two millions out there [in Petrograd], they are carrying the sense of responsibility for Petrograd, Russia. They are trying soberly, anxiously, conscientiously to govern Russia right, for themselves, for all of them, all. And that's democracy, isn't it?' "[9] Since the weakness Steffens saw in the United States government lay essentially in the distance between the politicians and the people, he was mightily impressed by a system in which the people, quite literally and directly, decided every move. The chaos of the situation seemed irrelevant when measured against the potential it held for improvement of mankind's lot. The important thing was that business had lost power and the people were righteously demanding democracy.

After his short stay in Russia, Steffens spent most of 1918 writing a few small pieces on the Russian Revolution and the bulk of his time crossing the United States lecturing on the revolution and its implications. But he could no longer count on the success he had once experienced with audiences. The war-conscious nation had deserted its liberalism, leaving Steffens far to the left. The McNamara case and the Mexican Revolution seemed tame when compared to his advocacy of the "anarchy" going on in Russia. His reputation was totally lost, except among the intelligentsia and radicals. His speeches were not well received and his articles, by and large, were rejected.

Immediately after the war Steffens sailed for Paris and the Peace Conference. He had great hopes that Wilson could accomplish a lasting peace, since he felt that the Russian Revolution had clearly pointed the direction any liberal would take into the future. The old "System" held tenaciously, however, each Frenchman and Englishman hoping for spoils from Germany. Unable to allay a general fear held by the governments of most of the Western world of an impending worldwide "red terror," the peace Wilson sought became, as is well known, a reactionary tragedy. The chances for a new world order were betrayed in favor of European (and probably American) imperialistic designs and punitive revenge.

In the years since Steffens had visited Russia the government he had first observed had been overturned. The new "red" government was even more radical than the deposed "white" government had been. Thus, the implications involved with recognition were even more awesome to the reactionary, war-weary West. Hoping they could get away with recognizing at worst the old, out-of-power but less radical "whites," the Allies denied recognition to the government in power.

Since the new Russian government was not recognized by the peacemakers at Versailles, Steffens suggested to Colonel Edward M. House, Wilson's adviser, that a delegation be sent to Russia where some kind of peace arrangement could be made with the Bolsheviks. Since the Allies were unhappy about dealing with the possibility of intervention in Russian affairs, a sounding mission, kept discrete, offered at least an opportunity for progress without the politically disastrous requirements of complete recognition by the capitalistic West. Steffens convinced House that some attempt at personal negotiations would introduce a human and informed atmosphere to the essential dealings with the *de facto* government. A quasi-official commission, made up of William C. Bullitt, an American intelligence officer, Captain W. Petit of American intelligence, Bullitt's secretary, and Steffens, left for Russia.

Once in Russia the members of the mission met with the emerging leaders of the Bolshevik state, most important among them being Lenin. After seeing the new government, Steffens's already favorable opinion of revolutionary Russia swelled. Once he saw Lenin he was convinced that the use of dictatorial power, in the hands of a confirmed Communist idealist and realist, was essential to a successful culmination of the revolution. As long as the dictator did not lose sight of his altruistic vision, the faith that the previously bumbling masses placed in him was laudable, in fact essential for progress. When he returned to Paris, Steffens summarized his conviction about the meaning of the revolution in a famous statement which he repeated in various forms to countless people for the rest of his life: "I have seen the future, and it works."[10]

While things appeared hopeful in Russia, chances for constructive use of the understanding the Bullitt Mission achieved were soon lost at Versailles. Afraid of political repercussions from a reactionary electorate, and facing what appeared to be greater problems that effectively ruled out the possibility of a compromise on Russian policy, the liberal forces at the conference—Wilson and Lloyd George—bowed to pressure from the conservative Clemenceau and denied their involvement with the Bullitt Mission. Steffens, more "red" than ever, withdrew politically from the situation. As in the McNamara case, the opportunity had been lost because of conservative reaction.

Steffens did not, however, become inactive. Although he had continued his relationship with the California woman for several years, he had met a young London economics student, Ella Winter, with whom he fell in love soon after his return from Russia. She was about a third his age, but he was attracted by her inquisitive and fresh approach, qualities he would have had a hard time finding in anyone his own age. As he traveled about Europe he wrote letters to her which trace his growing affection. Although he was plagued by a sense of responsibility toward his other love, she eventually became the victim of the evolving triangle. He visited Miss Winter (whom he affectionately called "Peter") in England until his visa was revoked, probably because of Lloyd George's fear of Steffens's ability to implicate him in the ill-fated Bullitt Mission.

A comparison of Steffens's marriage to Ella Winter, which came in mid-1924, with his first marriage reveals something of the changes that had occurred in his character (and, no doubt, in his cultural surroundings). When he married for the first time, he did so secretly. Living at that time in the Bohemian

Latin Quarter of Paris while attending college, he and his girl had slipped off quietly to England on what appeared to their friends to be a romantic vacation. They stayed only long enough to meet the residency requirements for marriage. When they returned to Paris married, they told no one of their wedding and thus had, as Steffens put it, "all the advantages of the law and all the thrills and prestige of lawlessness."[11] They successfully satisfied their desire both to conform to their own moral codes and to appear liberated from them.

However, Steffens argued against his second marriage, even after he knew that he was to be the father of Peter's child. While he loved her and was more than willing to stay with her, he rejected the requirements of the society he had rejected. But he was not a revolutionary in action or manners as much as in philosophy, and soon agreed it was best to marry, ending his arguments with the suggestion that immediately following the marriage they be divorced so that the pregnant young girl could claim to have been married and Steffens would still hold his freedom. But, for all practical and living purposes, the couple was happily married. Several years later, after their return to the United States, when Peter mentioned to a lawyer friend of hers that Steffens periodically suggested that she obtain a secret divorce from him so as to free both of them from legal ties, he started legal proceedings. When the petition for divorce, which was half a joke, mistakenly reached the press, the idea was dismissed, although even then Steffens tried to persuade his wife that such would be a better state of affairs.

With his new wife Steffens entered vigorously into the cultural milieu of Europe in the 1920's. During their courting days Steffens and Peter had joined an intellectual circle that boasted such members as Ezra Pound, Ernest Hemingway, Gertrude Stein, James Joyce, and two of Steffens's closest friends, Jo Davidson, the sculptor, and his wife Yvonne. His wife's circle of acquaintances included several leading English Socialists, most notably H. G. Wells.

Late in 1924 Steffens's only son, Pete Stanley Steffens, was born at the new residence of his parents in San Remo, Italy. The effect of fatherhood on Steffens was devastating. His writing from 1924 on is filled with concerns for and speculations about the world in relation to the coming generation. Mabel Dodge, a friend since prewar days, noted the effect of young Pete on his father when she compared his attitude before and after the boy's birth: "He was always free then [1910–14] because he did not know how to love. He learned later when Pete, his little boy, was born."[12] The correctness of Miss Dodge's observation is far more telling than it first seems to be. While Steffens had been married before and had loved and respected both his wife and his own family, there is a flavor and tone in his letters after Pete's birth that was wholly missing until then. Until 1924 Steffens had lived a footloose life, doing what he wished, too agile to be trapped by responsibilities. After Pete's birth he became a devoted, almost doting, father.

His role, in fact, was somewhat reversed with that of his wife. She was a young and energetic journalist working diligently on a career, while her husband had already achieved fame and was more than content to devote his energy and attention to his son. Acting more like a grandfather than a father, he carefully saw to it that young Pete would not be trapped by all the snares of "the System" that he, as a young man, had been unaware of. Pete was to be unencumbered by the ingrained prejudices and outdated dictums of society; he was going to be his own man. And so the one-time muckraker turned his attention to the educational process "the System" had used to perpetuate itself.

In 1927 Steffens and his family moved to the United States, eventually settling in Carmel, California, amid a small colony of artists and writers including the poet Robinson Jeffers and the novelist John Steinbeck. Concerned with the process of growing as it would influence Pete, Steffens turned inward, using his own life and experience as a case study. This analysis, which he had begun in Europe, was completed in late 1930 with the final chapter of his two-volume *Autobiography,* one of the best American autobiographies ever written. Steffens interpreted his entire life as a process of unlearning the ingrained moral and social codes forced upon him by the preceding generation. If he had produced nothing else, the *Autobiography* alone would earn him a position in the history of American politics and letters.

The publication of the *Autobiography* in 1931 caused an overnight rejuvenation of Steffens's long-lost public eminence. The United States was suffering from the depression, and the old muckraker's liberal and radical leanings no longer earned him scorn as they had in the boom years of the 1920's. Suddenly Steffens appeared as a prophet, a man who had not been fooled by Harding "normalcy" or Coolidge prosperity. A generation of prodigal sons, nursed on progressivism but lured away by reactionary fear and easy wealth, the public saw Steffens much as an indulgent and forgiving father figure, complete with a young son happily bouncing on his knee.

Part of the reason for his new popularity, no doubt, was Steffens's optimistic outlook for America. Although he had left his home a disappointed man, when Steffens returned to America he sensed a new wave of progress, a gentle mixture of capitalism and socialism. The problems of his generation were gone; labor was no longer striving for survival, and with the second Roosevelt the government was once again in liberal hands. The depression, while harsh, had illustrated the weaknesses of "the System" as it swept that system away, and the new America that was emerging had learned from its tragic past. To an old friend he wrote, "Capitalism is breaking down. One can see it from anywhere. And it's enough for me that our children are to grow up in a new and, I am sure, a better world: not yet free, but not hungry and not fearful."[13]

Steffens returned to Europe once after moving to the United States, spent one summer lecturing at a college in Colorado, and took several lecture tours. Once the *Autobiography* was finished, he approached his life as if a burden had been removed from his shoulders; he had done his duty and the rest of life could be a happy vacation. He took great pleasure in young and curious students, anxious that they be freed of traditional biases. He exercised fully his penchant for seeing the ironic in every situation. In a sense he grew happy with a world that had theretofore always been a disappointment.

Partially, of course, young Pete can be credited with changing his father's views. But credit should also be given to his country. Steffens was essentially an American, and as much as he had been intellectually comfortable in Europe, he had himself been something of a prodigal son. He was delighted that his homeland gave him new hope. For years he had been approaching his own form of communism much as a dogma, perhaps the only dogma he ever seriously suffered from, and when he found that America didn't need his lesson he happily laid down the burden. In his own country, with a bright future, he enjoyed the happiness of a man who had worked honestly and accomplished something meaningful.

Returning from a lecture tour in the East in the fall of 1933, Steffens suffered an attack of coronary thrombosis. While the illness caused him to remain at home, it did not affect his thinking or limit his friendships. Friends often visited, and young Pete brought him constant delight. Every day he wrote a short release for the local paper, usually recalling an incident or pointing out some irony in the news. Occasionally he produced a book review, and he continued mailing a steady stream of letters to friends around the world. His interest in liberal causes, in art, in the people, in youth, and in democracy never faltered.

On August 8, 1936, at the age of seventy, Steffens wrote the foreword to a new book containing many of his newspaper sketches and other articles that had appeared since the *Autobiography.* He began with this sentence: "When I finished my Life, I did not die as I might gracefully have done. I lived on and, of course, I learned and unlearned as always. Breathing the news was a habit by this time. So was changing my mind. And teaching. All were life habits."[14] The next afternoon, August 9, 1936, Steffens died, his last words to his doctor being, "No, no, I can't—"[15] Since he had requested that no institutional ceremony take place, his wife held an informal gathering of his friends before Steffens's burial in his family's plot in San Francisco. At that gathering John O'Shea, an Irish painter, told young Pete, "He was a great man, your Daddy, Pete." Pete turned to the artist and replied, "Yes, I'm beginning to see that. I thought he was just my Daddy and wrote a book."[16]

CHAPTER 2

Student

Education for an Active Life

S ACRAMENTO was an exciting city in the seventies. Past the boom of the gold rush days, it was still in the center of a relatively open frontier. On one hand were the excitement and adventure of a growing metropolis and state capital, with all the challenges and problems that would occupy many of Steffens's adult years; on the other hand was the wilderness, which had been the wellspring of much of the independence in American character. In 1893 historian Frederick Jackson Turner would note the significance of these two forces—the city and the frontier—in his famous thesis. Young Steffens, who titled the story of his childhood "A Boy on Horseback," knew both worlds.

While always a city boy by both nature and training, Steffens's familiarity with the frontier provided him with an understanding of some aspects of American character that other Americans of the twentieth century seem blind to. He maintained, for example, that his ownership of a horse was one source of his insights about emerging urban American society. The social and business instincts that came so naturally to most urbanites were observable traits to Steffens. Of his ownership of that pony he later wrote in his *Autobiography,* "After that blessed pony loped into my life, I never played those trading games which, as I see them now, are the leads not merely to gambling but to business. For there goes on among boys an active trade in marbles, tops, knives, and all other tools and properties of boyhood. . . .My theory is that those games are the first lessons in business: They cultivate the instinct to beat the other fellows. . . .I never got that training. . . ."[1] With his pony he escaped the crowd, with all its "herding habits of mind." He rode off alone, out of the vanishing frontier and into the emerging culture—always independent. His courage must have been sharpened in those years, for he never flinched at facing the unknown; he was always unruffled by social disfavor. In later life he would ride off alone into corrupt cities and states, into bloody revolutions, and often into the face of public scorn, without the slightest concern for the opinion of his fellows or for his own safety.

For a time in his childhood an older boy, Charlie Marple, came to live in the Steffens home while serving as a page in the California legislature. Charlie Marple introduced the school-trained, idealistic young Steffens to the railroad-controlled government of his state. Steffens's mental picture of an honorable, democratic government was shattered. "I saw," he later wrote,

> that the legislature wasn't what my father, my teachers, and grown-ups thought; it wasn't even what my histories and other books said. And Charlie took it as it was; my father took it as it seemed to be; I couldn't take it at all. What troubled me most, however, was that they none of them had any strong feeling about the conflict of the two pictures. I had. I remember how I suffered; I wanted, I needed, to adjust the differences between what was and what seemed to be. There was something wrong somewhere, and I could not get it right and nobody would help me.[2]

Thus disenchantment with existing government came early to Steffens. His was a complex problem; he knew and respected a man in the California government who others had said was a crook, and yet he knew he could depend on that man. His childhood taught him, among other things, that life was not as it appeared, that definitions—of good and evil, of right and wrong—were often misplaced, and that the remedy for social ills was far more complex and elusive than most contemporary critics were supposing.

In terms of the strict and formal education of his day, young Steffens must not have been a superior student, for after finishing his secondary education in a military academy in 1884 he failed his entrance examinations for the University of California at Berkeley. This failure, however, was most fortunate. Because of it, his father enrolled him with a private tutor, Mr. Evelyn Nixon, an Englishman schooled at Oxford, who had come to San Francisco for reasons of health. While tutoring his young charge, Nixon introduced the wayward student to "the world of conscious culture," as Steffens later labeled it.

The World of Conscious Culture

Evelyn Nixon transformed Steffens into a student, in the best sense of the word, by sharpening the youth's naturally inquisitive tendencies. Along with a group of Oxford and Cambridge expatriates in San Francisco the young Englishman devoted every Saturday evening to conversation, to "the free, passionate, witty exchanges of studied minds as polished as fine tools." Steffens merely observed, and he learned a major lesson for any scholar; of those evenings he later wrote:

Those conversations, so brilliant, so scholarly, and so consciously unknowing, seemed to me, silent in the background, to reveal the truth that even college graduates did not know anything, really. Evidences they had, all the testimony of all the wise men in the historical world on everything, but no decisions. . . . My head, busy with questions before, was filled with holes that were aching voids as hungry, as painful, as an empty stomach.[3]

Thus, when he entered Berkeley the next year he was a different kind of student. The humdrum mediocrity of typical college life, the posing of fraternities, the dullness of recited lectures and answers, the standardization of knowledge, the limitations of job-oriented goals, and the dryness of tone given to knowledge in academe all came to him as a dreadful disappointment. He had hoped that college would be an intellectual utopia. For the rest of his life he was critical of the way most schools functioned, standardizing thought and, he believed, creating social mediocrity via the curriculum. Education should elevate the social and intellectual plane, he felt, not perpetuate the status quo. His thoughts on most colleges and the stagnation they engendered in American society are echoed in his reflections about his years at Berkeley. "Knowledge," he wrote, "was absolute, not relative, and it was stored in compartments, categorical and independent. The relation of knowledge to life, even to student life, was ignored, and as for questions, the professors asked them, not the students; and the students, not the teachers, answered them—in examinations."[4] As he was later to discover of governments, universities were often responsible for initiating and fixing exactly those things they should have cured—narrowness of mind and a lack of inquisitive sensibilities.

Nonetheless, Steffens had been motivated by the example Evelyn Nixon set for him, and when a professor gave him the opportunity to "dig deeper" into a subject, he turned to the library and discovered there the great controversy of knowledge. In those subjects he enjoyed he flourished, gaining the friendship and admiration of his professors. In the subjects he disliked—or, to be specific, those he had not yet discovered the usefulness of—he faltered. Most specifically, in subjects related to ethics and philosophy he gained a burning desire to know more. A few of his professors at Berkeley did their work well. "I was stunned," Steffens recalled, "by the discovery that it was philosophically true, in a most literal sense, that nothing is known; that it is precisely the foundation that is lacking for science; that all we call knowledge rested upon assumptions which the scientists did not accept; and that, likewise, there is no scientific reason for saying, for example, that stealing is wrong. In brief, there was no scientific basis for ethics."[5] When he finished his baccalaureate in history at Berkeley, Steffens disappointed his father by refusing to go into business—his father offered him an interest in a San Francisco newspaper—and setting sail for Europe and the "high priests" of ethics at German universities.

Quality American graduate schools were in embryonic

stages when Steffens, tracing the steps of such earlier American intellectuals as George Bancroft and Henry Adams, journeyed to German universities in quest of an ethical foundation for knowledge. Like those preceding him, the young Californian was to gain insights from his first European odyssey that markedly improved his ability to analyze his native land. As his horse had removed him from some of the social forces forming the American business viewpoint, so his European experience saved him from American business-oriented philosophy during those few habit-forming years that follow a young man's graduation from sheltered academe. Steffens, who matriculated in ethics when he arrived in Berlin in 1889, was surely aware of Locke's theories on human understanding, and he took every opportunity to see that experience would imprint an expansive and question-filled picture on his receptive mind. He indulged his lusts, more interested in education than a degree, and thus he learned much.

Looking over some of his letters to his family and friends from those years, one can trace his intellectual growth. They detail the extremely wide range of his interests and reading. While obviously still suffering from a somewhat inflated ego, he was beginning to realize the extent of the task he had set for himself. "I am ploughing through a 15-volume edition of Greek history, besides my regular work, and in that I read several different authors every day. . . . This being in German takes more time," the young student wrote, showing off a little to his admiring sister.[6] To improve her education he advised her that after a few introductory works by Plato—"In the *Crito,* I believe it is, he demonstrates that goodness produces happiness. Follow him closely in this"—she might enjoy Matthew Arnold.[7]

Infatuated by the opera and aspiring artists, he studied orchestra scores of coming musical events with a young musician he met in Leipzig and, in Munich, debated "the everlasting question: 'Well, and what is art anyhow?' " with every young artist willing to debate.[8] He haunted art galleries, ancient ruins and standing castles, cathedrals, and museums. He laid the foundation for a life of cultural curiosity by approaching all the old, unanswerable questions with wide-eyed vigor and interest. He was, in the best sense of the phrase, an "innocent abroad," and he saw with a new American vision things the Europeans were themselves missing.

While measurement is impossible, Steffens's student years in Europe can hardly be overrated. Not only did they sharpen his already keen perception, but they gave him time once again to partake of the world of "conscious culture." Not that he found the universities there that superior; only that he was himself in the mood to get the most from experience, and did. Art, music, conversation, and a world of intellectuals dealing with artistic and unanswerable questions thrived in the student centers of Europe, and in that atmosphere the door Evelyn Nixon had unlocked was flung open. It is little wonder that liberal causes that alienated most provincial Americans as the twentieth century progressed always seemed too moderate to Steffens. America, when he returned, was an experiment for his philosophically and scientifically trained mind to dissect. While he was never capable of scientific detachment in those things he analyzed, his commentary always illustrated an ability to see the painfully obvious and significant elements of native American culture that home-trained analysts were blind to.

Philosophical Foundations for a Critic

And so, Steffens began seeking an ethical foundation for knowledge. Fully intending to wander from subject to subject as his quest demanded, he initiated his studies with Hegelian philosophy. But the categorization of traditional philosophic studies, like similar categorization in university life, was not allowed to mislead him. He gained what he could from Hegel and then happily moved on, careful to take as many interesting sidetracks as possible.

He started his study of Hegel in Berlin, then moved to

Heidelberg, where he listened attentively to Hegelian Professor Kuno Fischer. It is easy to understand how the Hegelian Dialectic—the process of eliminating false elements of a doctrine by combining that doctrine with the best elements of its refutation, and then repeating the process with the resulting doctrine over and over—influenced Steffens's method of analysis. It is still easier to see how Hegel's exceedingly abstract and philosophic arguments—perhaps more removed from observation and experience than any other philosopher's—would soon seem senseless. Steffens's American background was with him in Europe as his European training was to be with him in America. His abandonment of abstract philosophy was totally within the American mainstream. Thomas Jefferson, also versed in European philosophies, once wrote a young relative, "I think it is a lost time to attend lectures on moral philosophy. He who made us would have been a pitiful bungler if He had made the rules of our moral conduct a matter of science." In the tradition of most Americans, Steffens soon joined those who looked on complex metaphysics and philosophy with disdain—a pastime for those who have nothing really important to do. Hegel had little practical application. The society that had produced William James, who was then revolutionizing philosophic thought in America with pragmatism, had also produced Steffens. Philosophy was necessary and to be respected, but it had to aim at functional conclusions. Hegel's brand of ethics seemed almost opposed to either conclusions or application. There had to be something else, something that still dealt with the abstract and yet simultaneously gave tangible plans for social improvement.

Psychological Foundations for a Critic

Psychology offered a possible answer. A new science, it was directly related to human observation and thus human problems; it also offered a chance to find a framework upon which human intelligence was ordered. Leaving Heidelberg, Steffens took up his studies in Leipzig, where he enrolled in the classes of Whilhelm Max Wundt, a towering figure in the early years of experimental psychology. The Wundtians preached that the only way to study thought was through its behavioral manifestations, such as language and actions. The examination of one's own motives, determined through clinical observation and self-examination—"classical introspection" is the philosophic term—could help in leading to an understanding of society in general, and society's motives (and possibly ethics) in specific.

The greatest single thing Steffens gained from the experience was a scientific method of reasoning and observation. Rather than relying on fixed criteria formed through idealism and social education in a particular society in later years, Steffens would first observe America with the cold eyes of a scientist, and then, as a scientist rather than an emotional patriot, offer suggestions for its reform based on realistic motives and ideals in line with existing conditions. Logic and practicality were to be the watchwords of reform.

The Seeds of Muckraking

Steffens's letters from Germany and Paris are laced with observations on the nature of American society. Within three months after his arrival he wrote his mother that "the whole view [of life] is different and in the main the weight of common sense is on the German side. . . . An American gets so that he must work to keep him contented. His *whole* mind is on business and he becomes a harp with one string, the others withered and useless. . . . But one cannot understand this until he enters a nation where the spirit is different."[9] Clearly the influence of German society was to play a part in his later social observations. Early the next year he complained to a student friend still attending Berkeley that "there is something radically wrong in the system of education of which we

[Americans] are so proud."[10] On the subject of American politics and society, he communicated to his father, in a letter
from Leipzig, an idea that would later become a key factor in
his political philosophy: "It is disgraceful," he wrote, ". . . to be
'solid' for any party. It denotes intellectual lethargy and un-
patriotic indifference."[11]

And yet, throughout his journey he remained aware of the
promise of his homeland. While commenting on the government in Italy he assured his father, "Do not misunderstand
me. I wouldn't see an exchange of ours for any constitution in
Europe, but I mean that the men who are given the general
power [here] do more for their pay for the general
welfare. . . ."[12] This excerpt shows the seedling stage of
Steffens's later belief that the written form of government had
little to do with the actual nature of government in action.

All things totaled, there are several factors in his European
education that contributed to Steffens's later ability as a journalist. First, his training in ethics taught him to constantly consider the moral and ethical implications involved in his work.
His reporting was to go far beyond facts and personalities; it
would analyze the present with implications for the future. In
his muckraking, for example, Steffens wanted to find why
governments declined, and was not satisfied with knowing
merely who corrupted them and how. His journeys into Mexico and Russia, in a sense, were in pursuit of answers to a
philosophic question that had plagued him for years: how can
man best govern himself? As a reformer, he wanted to know
not only how to reform, but what would replace that which he
criticized if change actually was implemented. Further, he
reassessed the very terms by which men judged their fellow-
men; "bad" and "good" took on new meanings when he considered their implications within his ethical framework. Historian Otis L. Gratham has listed Steffens as "perhaps best
remembered" of those "men who had rejected the Victorian
code in their personal lives and had no thought of applying it
to America's social problems. [He] preferred to apply science,
or at the very least, rationality, rather than the Bible or
tradition."[13]

Second, his training in clinical psychology taught him to observe with scientific method and accuracy. Cities became mazes, and men were mice to be observed. While always sympathetic toward his subjects, Steffens maintained ruthless objectivity in his observations and conclusions, as often as not coming out in support of the man he was supposed to have attacked. While he acted with a specific goal in mind—which seems highly unscientific—he never compromised his conclusions. Indeed, some of the people he most liked were those he roasted over his inquisitor's flame, and he often became impatient with the reformers his journalism aided. His writing was based on more than intuition, moralism, or patriotism. Old assumptions were abandoned, new premises established, and new conclusions reached. While scientific method was not new, psychology gave new insights into human motivation; and while Steffens always saw the larger society in his analysis, he always saw it as a backdrop for individuals.

Third, his training in varied subjects—art, music, theater, ethics, history, philosophy, psychology, and languages—gave him a keen eye with which to scrutinize the American and later the world scene in depth. Steffens was an intellectual, constantly aware of new social currents changing his environment. When he finally published his *Autobiography* in 1931, he amazed everyone by the breadth of his experiences and interests. "No American of his time," according to historian Arthur Schlesinger, Jr., "seemed to have known so many famous people, asked so many searching questions, covered so many crises, or written so vividly about the twentieth century. And no American had so tirelessly assayed the possibilities of liberalism."[14] Even in his old age, he remained active in the liberal movements of the times. He never allowed himself the restrictions of categorization, with the exception of his constant liberalism.

Finally, his European experience put America into a fresh light. Separation made him aware of numerous unique features of the American scene and system that went unnoticed by most local critics. His European education saved him from that unreasonable sense of chauvinism that infected so many during Steffens's times. Capitalism, for example, never seemed sacred to him, nor did many of the restrictive elements of the Puritan ethic. He saw questions others missed and found answers they ignored.

CHAPTER 3

Journalist

Newspapers, Magazines, and the
Emergence of Modern America

NEW York City, where Steffens debarked upon his return from Europe, was alive with action in the 1890's. The center of America's ever-expanding economic life, the port through which a seemingly unending stream of immigrants entered, it was the living symbol of a transformation going on across the country. The twentieth century, with all its chaos and all its promise, was at hand, and nowhere could its conflicting elements be so clearly seen as in New York.

Newspapers were at the core of the transformation. Two giants of journalism and marketing, Joseph Pulitzer and William Randolph Hearst, had invaded the city from the adventurous West, forcing their indelible imprint on the nature of news. Anxious to increase their profits and aware of the need for change, they rushed to fill a vacuum created by the growing impersonal attitude of urban civilization. Newspapers no longer merely reported news and passed editorial comment on local, state, and national events. As Richard Hofstadter has pointed out, the newspapers "found themselves undertaking the more ambitious task of creating a mental world for the uprooted farmer and the villagers who were coming to live in the city."[1] While serving that function, they were themselves becoming big business and were part of the increasingly active and chaotic world they reported. Aside from reporting news, journalists created news and news events by creating or encouraging dramatic situations. If Hearst or Pulitzer wished to increase circulation, they fanned the fires of public interest by harassing a foreign power into a war or sponsoring a car race—and watched sales skyrocket as they reported the event.

The effects of this increased activity in journalism were numerous. A list of the reporters from that era would include most of the best-known names in literature of the realistic and naturalistic style. Hearst's *Journal* and Pulitzer's *World,* locked in a battle for primacy of circulation, forced the other New York papers either to adapt to new criteria of journalism or to close in failure. Some, like James Gordon Bennett, Jr.'s *Herald* and *Evening Telegram,* walked a tightrope between sensationalism and responsible reporting; others, like Charles A. Dana's *Sun,* which stood by the virtues of its writers, and Adolph Och's *Times,* which sponsored scientific exploration and instigated close ties to governmental (and thus insider's) information, adjusted along more respectable, traditional lines. Newspapers evolved quickly to a form roughly similar to today's papers.

But, through it all, E. Lawrence Godkin's *Evening Post* remained above the fracas. It neither courted nor cared for massive circulation, content to influence the leaders of finance, industry, and state. Its audience was select; Godkin led public opinion rather than pandering to it on the theory that the leaders of society read his paper and the rest of society followed them. Those changes that did occur in the *Post* came as a result of internal subversion by dissenting underlings rather than from editorial direction. Occasionally some young reporter or editor might gradually insert a little crime or police news, but never did its extent approach similar subject-matter coverage in competing papers. All change was subtle, and never immediately noticeable.

While the late nineteenth century was a period of rapid evolution for newspapers, it was a period of revolution for magazines. They expanded on a national scale as newspapers did on a local scale. Rarely have so many things converged in the development of one industry: postal rates fell, Rural Farm Delivery (R.F.D.) expanded, high speed presses were perfected with resultant cost reductions, photographic reproduction improved and cheapened, national industries demanding national advertising campaigns emerged, the literacy rate multiplied, and leisure time made self-education attractive. All these factors contributed to making magazines part of the average citizen's daily life. When Frank Munsey, of *Munsey's Magazine,* discovered he could make the lion's share of his profits and expenses from advertising, he started a subscription and newsstand price reduction cycle emulated by numerous new periodicals seeking larger markets; included among the new entries on the market were the *Ladies' Home Journal, Cosmopolitan,* and *McClure's.*

Older, tradition-bound magazines like *Harper's* and *Scribner's,* costing considerably more, were content with small audiences of genteel readers. They selected their content with little concern for popular tastes. The newer magazines, on the other hand, were edited with the mass public taste constantly in mind, and their circulation soared, until monthly sales as high as one million were not uncommon. The impact and importance of these journals rose proportionately with their audience. An exposé in *McClure's,* for whom Steffens was to work, was widely read, and repercussions from articles became significant in terms of politics. Magazines forced national affairs—political, social, industrial, and intellectual—into the spotlight, acting something like a newsmagazine today, but with greater impact. The expansion of critical newsmagazines, of course, increased the knowledge of the voting and purchasing public, and thus was to be a central factor in the extent of the muckraking movement.

The tie of reform to newspapers at the local level was echoed by the tie of reform to magazines at the national level. "To an extraordinary degree," Hofstadter suggests, "the work of the Progressive movement rested upon its journalism. . . . It is hardly an exaggeration to say that the Progressive mind was characteristically a journalistic mind."[2]

Aimed at large audiences, these new magazines, though limited in depth, were hardly indications of an inactive or intellectually narrow public mind. They bustled with activity. A content analysis of any one of them, from the *Ladies' Home Journal* to *Cosmopolitan,* would reveal a wide audience interest in scientific advancement, history, the beaux arts, and public affairs.

Newspaper Days

Steffens's first job after returning from Europe was with the *New York Post.* Had it been with one of the more flamboyant journals, it is questionable what the nature of his later writing would have been, but his experience on the *Post* instilled in him the key virtues of good journalism. Starting as a general reporter, he worked a number of beats and learned the practical aspects of finding and writing newsworthy stories.

After he had proved himself an able general reporter, his first specialized assignment was as a substitute Wall Street—or business and finance—reporter, a job he ably mastered during the panic year of 1893. The seeds of his disenchantment with the business elite in America can be traced to that experience. "Men of exaggerated success," he wrote to an old friend, "like Russell Sage, J. Pierpont Morgan, President Williams of the great Chemical Bank, President Maxwell of the New Jersey Central Railroad, these and other men who have succeeded by dint of their own efforts, excelling others in large enterprises requiring intellectual powers of some kind, are all, all incapable of logical thought *even in* business matters. . . . They simply feel that such a thing will go. They do not reason it out carefully."[3]

Steffens advanced rapidly. Natural curiosity, energy exhibited in performing his work, a keyed-up intellectual grasp applied in understanding the total implications of seemingly minor stories, the gift of winning the admiration and trust of men in high places who were significant as news sources, and the natural, undefinable instincts of a good news reporter combined to make Steffens one of the *Post*'s most valuable men.

When Steffens's immediate boss at the *Post* decided to discretely insert some police news into the paper—a type of news that Godkin shunned—he felt he would most likely succeed by tying it in with the details of the work of a municipal reformer, Reverend Charles Parkhurst—a type of news Godkin promoted. Steffens was selected to accomplish this subtle sabotage, and was given an office across the street from the police station where he could watch events firsthand. His reaction to the assignment explains his success. Hearing of his new job, he described to his father what he would be doing. "It is beastly work," he wrote, work dealing with "police, criminals, and low-browed 'heelers' in the vilest part of the horrible East Side amid poverty, sin and depravity. Will it degrade me? Will it make a man of me? Here is my field, my chance. Wright [Steffens's editor] says he does not know that I shall get there, but he says I will if anyone on his staff can. So it is begun."[4] In his *Autobiography* Steffens would later emphasize the value of his police reporting. No doubt it established a technique he found essential for the next twenty years. "Reporting at police headquarters," he recalled, "was like a college educaion in this, that one had to take several courses all together. There was the police news, police policies and politics; the Ghetto, with its synagogues, theaters, and moral struggles; the strikes; and, on the side, Wall Street. It differed from college in this, that I was interested in each of these courses and could see that they belonged together. They all contributed to the learning of life as it is lived."[5] The police beat was probably responsible for instilling in Steffens, who was something of an aristocrat by training and character, a sense of the flavor of daily life that is essential in journalism aimed at the masses.

Soon after being given the police beat Steffens had an opportunity to display his real worth. The United Press and the Associated Press—the major news services—were sources for most of the major daily papers. Although each service used three or four experienced men, the *Post*'s man, required to report his own story unaided by the new services, "scooped" the competition on several occasions.

Thus Steffens grew in talent and prestige. He competed

with what was probably the best group of reporters in the country, if not the world, finishing favorably. "The ablest all-round reporter on the staff," wrote fellow reporter Norman Hapgood in his memoirs, "was Lincoln Steffens, and I thought him also the best general reporter in the city. He was. . .interested primarily in events that passed before his eyes, with comment on their significance kept in the background, and narrative description, and humor combined with a professional thoroughness."[6]

Moving into Reform

Maintaining his ties with Wall Street, Steffens cautiously but quickly learned his duties as a police reporter. Making the seemingly logical assumption that the police were as anxious for reform as Reverend Parkhurst, the man he was covering, Steffens was stunned to find that, rather than lending support, the police were among Parkhurst's major foes.

Quickly making friends with the *New York Sun*'s reporter Jacob Riis, now famous for his early exposé of slum conditions entitled *How the Other Half Lives*, the idealistic young Steffens pieced together a realistic picture of New York's social order. Like Wall Street, the police station presented a false front. In reality, Steffens learned, the criminals and the police combined forces in order to make an organization that was efficient and beneficial for both sides. Police allowed crime within bounds in return for an orderly control of the situation and a share of the profits. Should some troublesome crime occur —one that would embarrass the police or the politicians in power—the forces of crime and of the law would unite, set the mistake in order, and create the image of an efficient, orderly police system. It was the best of all possible worlds for the parties concerned; the police gained, the criminals gained—only the public lost. And as long as knowledgeable reporters didn't blow the whistle, they were fed tips and leads that would allow them to "scoop" the other reporters while leading an easy, insider's way of life.

Reverend Parkhurst, however, was a thorn in the

organization's side. His calls for reform were a constant source of public attention and he refused to be bribed. The reporters did their best to help their cohorts in crime by painting the moderate reformer as a radical, but they could not afford to ignore him, especially after he acquired the *Post*'s support.

Business was America's god in the 1890's. That which promoted business was good; that which hindered it was not. Efficiency was good; good not only in obvious outlets of business, but good in every aspect of life. On Wall Street Steffens had learned that the corporate structure of most businesses was not efficient, since the law required certain restraints. But when business and the law differed, business came out ahead. In order to evade the law, a Wall Street lawyer, James B. Dill, organized an intricate system of business incorporation that New Jersey passed into law. Using the New Jersey system, businessmen were able to organize under ever fewer and increasingly efficient administrators, thus following the letter of the law and evading its spirit. The result, in final analysis, was the "trust." Efficiency demanded that competition be controlled or, if possible, eliminated. To ensure the appearance of free competition, businessmen established a facade of legality made up of directors—men who technically held power over the trusts. Steffens labeled these men "dummy directors." Real power was in the hands of an ever decreasing—and increasingly efficient—group of bankers. Business efficiency was replacing public responsibility.

Reverend Parkhurst was discovering the same curse in police affairs. On Mulberry Street, across from the police station, Steffens learned that the police were going through a similar evolution. There were police commissioners and officers for the public eye, but behind the front what they constituted was a highly efficient organization that combined both police and criminals into a functioning unit. As in business, the system was revolving increasingly around one man—"the boss"—who could administer more efficiently than boards of aldermen, police commissioners, and endless public stooges. But political efficiency was a step ahead of economic efficiency, and a single individual had emerged as "boss."

Mr. Richard ("Boss") Cocker held the center of political ac-

tivity in New York. He was not elected to any post, but was a
party man. Steffens, unsure of what was going on, approached Cocker for an interview. Much to his surprise, he
was impressed by and liked the man. (The same was true of
his experience with Dill, the lawyer responsible for the New
Jersey system, who had revealed the inside workings of Wall
Street to him.) The two men, Cocker and Steffens, had like
interests, and after the "Boss" was sure that he could speak
without being reported, he opened up to Steffens (as Dill had
done) and aided the reporter by giving him a unique viewpoint from which to analyze American civil government.

All this, however, was but the shadow of a system Steffens
would be studying for years to come. He did not yet clearly
perceive why various business interests seemingly desirous of
reform did not unite to eliminate political interests. Why did
they not support Dr. Parkhurst? " 'Ever heard that business is
business?' " Cocker asked him. " 'Well, so is politics business,
and reporting—journalism, doctoring—all professions, arts,
sports—everything is business.' "[7] Dill gave a similar answer
when Steffens asked him the same question. Dill kicked the
naïve young reporter's shin, and asked, " 'Why does your
mouth cry out when only your shin is hurt?' "[8] While still un-
stated, Steffens's later idea of a "System" overriding American
society is clearly evident in his newspaper work. The interdependence of all elements of society was a relatively new
concept, and Steffens was only beginning to grasp it.

Throughout this period he continued making friends from
both ends of the social spectrum—reformers and those in
need of reform. In general he respected men who were stead-
fast in their individual beliefs, regardless of what they were.
Virtue was to be found in individual strength, not in any
cause. Throughout life he remained reluctant to condemn individuals. Of one corrupt policeman, whom he later recruited
to the reformist persuasion, Steffens asked, "Isn't a strong
man, however bad, socially better than a weak man, however
good?"[9] It was society, he felt, that misdirected potentially vir-
tuous leaders, and an adjustment in society would be more

beneficial than a clean sweep of any particular group of wrongdoers. The politically adept bosses, he observed, "seem to be as eager to do great good as great evil. They simply are not asked to do good; the drift of things, the rewards, the applause and education are all the other way."[10]

Significantly, Steffens generally attacked organizations, not men. He felt that society as a unit was guilty; men as individuals could control their destinies to only a limited degree. Unlike his friend Roosevelt and numerous other reformers, he grew to believe that placing good men in government, or any social organ, would not necessarily solve any problems—but it could corrupt the good men. In fact, he decided in later years that the recruitment of the knowledgeable corrupt into the reform movement was essential for success. These converts, he stressed, would have the proven ability most reformers lacked—ability to make government function smoothly. How could a businessman, trained in an employer-employee relationship dependent on profit, step into a position in which he was to represent not self-interest but public interest, when his entire background had trained him in the principles of *caveat emptor*? It was not logical, and Steffens's philosophic training made him yearn for a logical approach. The business ethic in government was the source of the problem, not its cure; and people who understood this were more likely to be successful as reformers.

The Lexow Investigations

Meanwhile, Reverend Parkhurst's continual chipping away at the political bulwark came to fruition with the Lexow Police Investigations. The New York State legislature established a bipartisan commission in 1894 to investigate corruption in the New York City police. Originally those men "in the know" assumed that the police would be given a "whitewash" and the political dirty linens would be cleaned out of the public eye. The reformers, however, employed a particularly able young lawyer, William Travers Jerome, and he expertly glued public attention to the trials. "New York this time will not stop with one triumph," Steffens triumphantly wrote his father. "Everybody wants to go on, to keep up the fight and to exact from the elect what was refused by, and caused the defeat of, the overthrown."[11]

The victim of the investigation was, for a short while, the New York Tammany machine. A businessman mayor, William L. Strong, was elected by the reform forces. His administration, while soon lost in confusion, brought the appointment of a board of police commissioners that included a young aristocrat named Theodore Roosevelt, who quickly asserted his dominance by having himself elected president of the board. Totally unprepared for the job, but typically enthusiastic, Roosevelt forged ahead, learning what he could as he moved and bludgeoning his way through all he could not learn. To solve his lack of practical knowledge of New York's underworld and political system, he invited Riis and Steffens into his office and, in his forthright manner, asked, "Now, then, what'll we do?"[12] And so, along with his reporting work, Steffens gained an active though unofficial place on T.R.'s staff.

Steffens centered his efforts at active reform on a police officer, Captain Schmittenberger, who had confessed to the Lexow Committee all that he, as a bribe collector, had learned about the underside of the police department. Schmittenberger, after confessing, became one of New York's most effective policemen. Steffens convinced Roosevelt to use the reformed civil servant in the city's worst districts, where he proved extremely successful, much to the commissioner's suprise. Years later Steffens led a successful drive to have Schmittenberger made chief of police. In fact, Steffens was so fascinated by the crook gone straight that he attempted to write a novel based on his story, which he unfortunately never finished.[13]

The reform wave in New York soon waned and Tammany regained control. Steffens remained active, but he did not yet totally understand what caused the reformist downfall. And so, he turned his attention once again to art—in specific, the art of journalism.

The New York Commercial Advertiser

An established and highly respected reporter, Steffens was one of a group of men who left the *Post* in 1897 to take over the *New York Commercial Advertiser,* where he became city editor. A small and previously insignificant paper, the *Commercial Advertiser* became, under Steffens's leadership, a center for idealists and dreamers.

Most noticeable about it was its singularly impressive staff of writers. The number of successes that can be traced to the *Advertiser* attests to its value as a school for journalism. Among those who either began or improved their careers there were Guy Scull and Robert Dunn, who were later to become famous as war reporters; Abraham Cahan, later editor of the *Jewish Daily Forward,* the world's largest Yiddish paper; Carl Hovey, eventually editor of *Metropolitan Magazine;* and two brothers, Norman and Hutchins Hapgood—Norman became editor of *Collier's Weekly* and Hutchins, the more radical of the two, was to be associated with countless liberal causes for the rest of his life.

When he got control of his own paper, Steffens sent the word out to graduating classes of Harvard, Yale, Columbia, and other colleges that this was to be no typical newspaper, and that anyone wishing to experiment would be given a chance. "There were no rules about promptitude, sobriety, accuracy," he wrote, "no lists of friends or enemies of the paper; no editorial policy; no 'beats'; and best of all, there was no insistence even upon these rules, which were broken at any one's convenience."[14] Hutchins Hapgood remembered the paper as "a state of mind, so to speak," and reported that

Steffens's "interest when he became city editor was distinctly that of the artist." Hapgood paints a colorful picture of what work on the *Commercial Advertiser* under Steffens's direction was like:

Steffens in those days was not interested in sociological or political things; the reforming or revolutionary instinct had not taken possession of him. . . He felt keenly and in great detail the picturesque and amusing side of the life of the city. He liked articles so written that the reader could see, while getting the news, the background of men behind the news. A character sketch of a Tammany official, a teamster maliciously bumping into another teamster but so gently that nothing could be done about it, was an important event in Steffens's imagination, and he would take anything of this sort—what would be called by the other editors an eccentric story—and put it on the first page. For example, I interviewed a Tammany man who was the head of the Aquarium. [Tammany]. . .sneered at the chemical and other tests as to the fitness of the water for the fish. When I asked Colonel Jones how he found out whether the water was right for the fish he said that when the fish died he knew it wasn't good for them. Steffens treated this story as a matter of first importance; it occupied a prominent place on the first page. And, of course, it was a great political moment.[15]

The *Commercial Advertiser,* in short, resembled a hybrid of magazine and newspaper, with an emphasis on feature stories and items with artistic rather than pure news content.

Steffens's years there were ones of transition. While he exhausted himself and made a success of his endeavor, his mind was much occupied with the art of journalism. He wrote some fiction, which such periodicals as *Harper's* and *Chap-Book* accepted. The different areas he investigated on this innovative newspaper made him want to try new experiments. In late spring of 1901 both he and his wife, who suffered a serious lung illness, were given doctor's orders to get out of New York. They took an extended vacation in the Adirondacks.

At this point in his life Steffens had earned himself a reputation as both a journalist and a reformer. But he had not yet begun those things that would make him famous. When he returned from his rest, recovered and anxious to get to work, he

ers at fees varying according to the periodical and the reputation of the writer. In most cases this meant that anyone seeking a living from writing had little time for research, causing
magazines to shy away from articles that might be founded on
poorly substantiated information, making fiction the foundation of content. By hiring a staff, *McClure's* could and did demand extensive, painstaking research, from which it acquired
factually sound—and thoroughly sensational—results. Ida
Tarbell, for example, took about five years to complete her
series on Standard Oil, at a final cost of about four thousand
dollars an article. Steffens's articles averaged only half that in
cost, but he produced at a rate of about four a year.[19]
McClure's earned its reputation as the source of the muckrakers.

Because modern readers have a misconception of the term
"muckraking," it should be stressed that the "muckraking"
done by *McClure's* followed the highest traditions of American
journalism. Common misuse of the term by modern critics has
changed its meaning, until it is now often used when the
phrase "yellow journalism" would be far more appropriate.
The term "muckraking" was originally used by Bunyan in
Pilgrim's Progress to refer to those who never see anything but
the negative side of life. The modern usage of the term stems,
surprisingly enough, from its use by Theodore Roosevelt, who
applied it to the reform journalists in a speech heard by
members of the Senate, House, Supreme Court, Cabinet, and
foreign delegations on April 14, 1906. Roosevelt had political
reasons for attacking his friends in journalism, but his condemnation was far more drastic than necessary. It gave stalwarts a catchy phrase which they brandished with abandon
against their enemies, the Progressives. According to Steffens,
Roosevelt told him that he meant only to defend Senator
Chauncy Depew from the attacks in writer David Graham
Phillips's series entitled "The Treason of the Senate," but
Roosevelt's speech went way beyond that. Other writers have
demonstrated Roosevelt's premeditation; Ray Stannard Baker,
another *McClure's* writer, wrote to Roosevelt before the ad-

dress was given when he heard speculation about its content, asking that a clear distinction be made between irresponsible journalists writing for sensationalist purposes and reform journalists writing for ideological purposes.[20] He, like so many others, was to be unjustly condemned by a man who owed him a considerable debt. The day after the speech, Steffens told the President, "Well, Mr. President, you have put an end to all these journalistic investigations that have made you.' "[21]

Steffens was right; the term led to an unfair classification of the sensational and the reformist press under a single phrase. Whatever the cause, the modern reader should make this distinction: the work of the writers at *McClure's* (and at a number of other magazines labeled as "muckraking") was scrupulously researched, honestly presented, and largely reformist in purpose; the work of the "yellow journalists," on the other hand, often bordered on pure fiction, pandered to the most sensational sentiments, and was written to sell papers. (Also, it should be noted that "yellow journalism" was more prevalent in newspapers than in magazines.) While the so-called muckrakers had an avowed intent—reform—and wrote with something akin to an abolitionist's fervor, they had wholly honest and praiseworthy motives, and their product was, by and large, sound, reasonable, and interesting history.

CHAPTER 4

Muckraker

"The System"

T HE majority of the public writing Steffens produced in his muckraking period can be fitted into a single framework. Whether by design, internal logic, or coincidence, each of his articles is a building block, gaining support from the one before it and giving support to the one after it; together they form an impressive analysis of the structure to which Steffens gave the now famous label "the System."

The first block in "the System" is considered in the series of articles collected under the title *The Shame of the Cities*, a volume containing seven essays previously printed in *McClure's*, plus an "Introduction; and Some Conclusions," added to the beginning to underline the interrelation of the various articles. The premise behind the collection of all the articles in one book was that what was happening in individual cities was of interest to citizens across the nation; implicit in that assumption was the conviction, conscious or unconscious, that what was true in one city was true in most cities. Thus, the book promoted the theory that there was something natural in the development of local corruption that made it spring up wherever certain conditions were present. Each particular city, therefore, was to be seen as an example, not as a unique exception; descriptions were written to make the reader want to reform in his own city that element he had seen illustrated by the exposé of some other city.

The first city reviewed was St. Louis. Its Municipal Assembly, containing a City Council and a House of Delegates, was shown to contain a "combine," a group of men large enough

to be the deciding factor in any decision. This combine would
sell its services—votes—to the highest bidder. All of this soon
became institutionalized, a fact of government recognized by
all realistic businessmen desiring a share of the public wealth.
According to Steffens,

in order to insure a regular and indisputable revenue, the combine
of each house drew up a schedule of bribery prices for all possible
sorts of grants, such a list as a commercial traveler takes out on the
road with him. There was a price for a grain elevator, a price for a
short switch; side tracks were charged for by the linear foot, but at
rates which varied according to the nature of the ground taken; a
street improvement cost so much; wharf space was classified and precisely rated. As there was a scale for favorable legislation, so there
was one for defeating bills. It made a difference in the price if there
was opposition, and it made a difference whether the privilege asked
was legitimate or not. But nothing was passed free of charge.[1]

This rather lengthy excerpt gives some idea of the nature and
tone of Steffens's prose style when he was writing for the
magazine audience. The business advantages purchased (as
described above) existed in most urban areas. Thus, the
reader was immediately suspicious of his own local government. Spurred by Steffens's articles, local citizens across the
nation instigated municipal investigations.

It should be noted that each article centered on a reform
movement that had already exposed much of what Steffens
was reporting. While he was an able and diligent reporter,
and much of his information was previously unpublished (and
much that he found was never published), his articles did not
lead to reform in the specific cities he exposed; rather, they
told what the status quo was and who was responsible for
whatever reform was going on. Thus, Steffens was often asked
to come to cities that were undergoing reform where he could
use the information that was surfacing in those local investigations. The primary gain that came from his reporting was the
national prominence it lent to local reformers who were being
smeared by stalwart forces on the home front. While he aided
the reform movement by drawing national attention and pres-

sure to local reform and thus encouraged and inspired similar movements, he did not personally attempt to instigate a reform movement himself until several years later.

Credit for the reform movement, therefore, does not belong to the muckrakers. While their work gave invaluable and unmeasurable support, and no doubt deserves considerable credit for the degree reform succeeded, it was most definitely a case of reporting rather than instigating the news, with a few notable exceptions. Generally speaking, the magazines were reacting to a reformist desire deep within the public as a whole—one that was triggered by their revulsion against the state of civic affairs rather than by sensationalism or fanaticism. As historian Louis Filler states in his classic volume on the subject, "Had there been no one but Steffens, *The Shame of the Cities* would never have been written, let alone printed. Steffens was a son of his times."[2]

From St. Louis Steffens moved to Minneapolis. His article on that city revealed collusion between the police department and organized crime. The story was one of "a deliberate, detailed management of the police force, not to prevent, detect, or arrest crime, but to protect, share with, and direct the criminals. . . . [The Mayor] and the police force, with professional criminals to advise them, made a schedule of prices for the privilege of breaking the laws."[3] Steffens had known such a system in New York, and his discovery of a similar situation in another city lent support to his belief in the national, systematic nature of corruption. More support was gained for the theory when, before leaving Minneapolis, he discovered that there had been corruption on the board of aldermen there just as there had been in St. Louis. The pattern of corruption was expanding and becoming increasingly believable.

Consequently, he returned to St. Louis for his third article. Once there he learned quickly that, aside from the political corruption already exposed, St. Louis also suffered from organized police-criminal corruption just as Minneapolis did. In a general sense, he had laid the foundation of all that was to follow. Steffens later told his editor, S. S. McClure, "Evidently you could shoot me out of a gun fired at random and, wherever I lighted, there would be a story, the same way."[4]

His further articles in *The Shame of the Cities* merely illustrated the extent, causes, ramifications, strengths, weaknesses, and possible cures for the organized corruption. In his "Introduction; and Some Conclusions" to the volume he listed his findings as follows: "St. Louis exemplified boodle; Minneapolis, police graft; Pittsburg[h], a political and industrial machine; and Philadelphia, general civic corruption; so Chicago was an illustration of reform, and New York of good government."[5] It should be stressed that Steffens never exposed all he knew; he revealed only enough to illustrate the extent of the problem he faced. He said that he "picked out what light each [city] had for the instruction of the others. But, if I was never complete, I never exaggerated."[6] Thus, the first block in "the System" was itself a structure made of smaller units.

The second major block of articles was the series collected in the book entitled *The Struggle for Self-Government*. Soon after delving into civic corruption Steffens realized that curing corruption at local levels would require more than local-level exposure. The entire body politic, not just one part, would have to be exposed. States, Steffens decided, "were as bad or as good as their cities. . . . The State machine, whether of the same or a different party, would back the city machine; a corrupted State would defend the graft of a corrupted city."[7] This conclusion was, of course, only logical. Cities derived their power from states, and if reformers were ever to succeed they would have to eliminate the source of the infection.

The Struggle for Self-Government assessed the governments of six states: Missouri, Illinois, Wisconsin, Rhode Island, New Jersey, and Ohio. As in the case of the cities, most of the states muckraked were in the late stages of internal reform movements at the time they were analyzed, which was far from coincidental; Steffens planned his efforts to assist his ever-growing number of reformist friends.

The structure of the corruption studied was markedly familiar to his readers: merely city corruption on a state-wide scale. The first of the articles, "Enemies of the Republic: Missouri," was structured to lend support to a local reformer, Joseph W. Folk, whom Steffens had already aided in his first article on St. Louis. Folk had been forced to run for governor in order to gain a wider base of public support (the local machine he had attacked was too entrenched and had too many friends to be defeated at the local level) and attack the corruption at its root. The article contended that good business—that is to say, successful businessmen—had come to depend upon business control of the privileges granted by the state, such as laws regulating distribution, production standards, public saftey regulations, and so on. In order to secure laws favorable to their interests, businessmen bought legislators. The expansion of business, naturally, entailed a similar expansion of corruption.

The second article, "Enemies of the Republic: Illinois," illustrates how big business bypassed the city, going directly to the state when foiled by a local reform movement; the example offered by Illinois concerned a battle by financier Charles T. Yerkes to gain a street railway franchise in Chicago. Stopped by that city, he took over the still-corrupt state machine, which had great power of patronage and essentially determined all laws concerning the nature of local governments. Secondly, the article revealed that the so-called leaders of society—big businessmen and the social elite—were hindering reform efforts because big business had an interest in the state's business-political system.

The third article, "Enemies of the Republic: Wisconsin," illustrated the battle of one man against a corrupt state party organization. The man, Robert M. La Follette, was to become one of Steffens's heroes, a liberal beyond reproach. La Follette, aside from being almost inhumanly honest, was a constant democrat, drawing support from the grass roots of his state. Steffens's article told little that his readers did not know, at least in theory. Its major significance was that it introduced Steffens's readers to La Follete and Wisconsin, a state that was soon to be considered a model of liberal experimentation and reform. Throughout the early years of this century Steffens wrote several articles about various aspects of Wisconsin's government and its educational reform, both as models for other states and to lend political support to La Follette.

The next article, "Rhode Island, A State for Sale," did several things. First, it illustrated that the "better element" of society was responsible for corruption, not the immigrants and the undereducated, who were typically given the blame. Rhode Island had limited the franchise to a relatively elite class, and its constitution had been written in an undemocratic way that ensured that power remained in the hands of a very select few. So small was the voting public, in fact, that the bribe givers didn't buy the elected officials (as was usually true); they bribed the voters themselves to elect the men they already controlled. The people came cheap. Consequently, fault for Rhode Island's corruption lay with the voters—its theoretically safe natural aristocracy of established, educated citizens.

Second, Steffens gave evidence to show that the boss of the state—the man who distributed the bribe money and thus controlled elections—was the legal counsel for most of the state's big businesses. Obviously, he saw to it that the money he distributed worked to the advantage of his clients. This was but one illustration of the tie between big business and government corruption.

Finally, and probably most original and significant, the main business "the boss" represented was owned by three men, one of them being Senator Nelson Aldrich, the state's elder member of the national Senate, called by some the "political boss of the United States." It was Aldrich whom businessmen at the national level, such as J. P. Morgan, contacted when they needed cooperation in Washington. The next logical progression in Steffens's structure—from the state to the national level—was illustrated by the situation in Rhode Island; just as cities were tied to states, states were tied to the national machine. The organization Steffens was analyzing was, at last, brought to the national level.

The next article related how business interests had won out against democracy, at least in the state of New Jersey. The article, originally two installments long, detailed the evolution of the famous and controversial New Jersey trust laws, at just about the same time Steffens's old friend, the President, was attacking the giant trusts.

The trust laws had evolved out of big business's desire for efficiency. When other states passed consumer- and small-business-oriented legislation, big business turned to New Jersey, where laws sanctioned their monopolistic practices. Since states had to recognize each other's company charters, the New Jersey laws enabled the bypassing of most state-level business reform. New Jersey represented big business rather than the people, at the expense of the rest of the nation's citizens. The corruption and control of one state was thus shown to have significant national implications, and once again those implications hinted at a national disaster.

The final article, "Ohio, A Tale of Two Cities," told how a corrupt state legislature revoked the charter of a reformed city and substituted in its place a charter modeled on the charter of a city that was firmly in the hands of corrupt business influences. Once again, the ability of higher levels of government to thwart local reform was illustrated.

The third block in the structure was the federal government. By the time Steffens reached this point he had left *McClure's* and the *American*. In order to get published he had himself syndicated through a number of newspapers, including Joseph Pulitzer's *New York World* and *St. Louis Post-Dispatch*. President Roosevelt was influential in helping Steffens research the series; he gave the energetic young reporter a note containing the following instructions:

To any officer of or employee of the Government:
Please tell Mr. Lincoln Steffens anything whatever about the running of the government by or under offices of the Executive that you know (not incompatible with the public interests) and provided only that you tell him the truth—no matter what it may be—I will see that you are not hurt.

T. Roosevelt[8]

Three months later Roosevelt attacked liberal journalists, calling them "muckrakers," a name which he told Steffens (and several of his other friends) was not meant to apply to him.

It is unnecessary to detail the specifics of Steffens's exposures at the national level. Corruption was caused, organized, and maintained by methods similar to those already familiar to his readers. The significant implication was that the United States, at all levels of government, was no longer controlled by representatives responsive to the people who elected them. The corrupt portion of the organization—"the System"—was, at least as far as its governmental ramifications, exposed in its entirety.

Tangential and supportive to the groups of essays already mentioned were numerous other articles, mostly biographical sketches of reformers recounting their fights for reform, that expanded on and illustrated concepts already familiar to Steffens's readers. Most important among these articles were a number of biographies, later collected in a volume entitled *The Upbuilders,* published in 1909, and three other articles—"Roosevelt, Taft, La Follette," "Bryan, Johnson," and "Eugene V. Debs"—that appeared in *Everybody's Magazine* in the pre-election months of 1908.

The men analyzed in *The Upbuilders* were local or state reformers, the most interesting being Judge Ben Lindsey of Denver, who organized the first Juvenile Court. Lindsey's story interested Steffens because it concerned the effects of society on youth, and thus concerned the future as well as the present; because it illustrated that changing the treatment of misdirected boys would change their social behavior, thus supporting Steffens's notion that conditions, not people, were responsible for the state of society; and because of the character of Judge Lindsey, who was to become a close friend to Steffens. Like Steffens, Lindsey felt that genuine reform would require a massive and fundamental change in society. A determined and intellectual liberal, Lindsey was more concerned with compassion and the future than with justice; his reform eventually reached the gates of big business, which he considered the source of most of society's troubles and the ultimate factor in turning children to a life of crime, and it was with business that Lindsey, like Steffens, reached an impasse. Both of these men would, in later years, become confirmed radicals, turning to economic theories that illustrated the faults of capitalism.

The three articles containing the stories on the leading contenders for the nominations for the presidency are significant because they clearly illustrate Steffens's working to provide information essential for democracy to the mass public. The role of mass media in forming public opinion toward one national candidate and against another—a role accepted now without thought—was relatively new in 1908. Nationwide magazines of massive circulation were the first mass medium to span the entire nation on a pervasive and influential scale. The importance of magazine journalism in the workings of democratic society, while traceable to the beginnings of American society, increased greatly in the early years of the twentieth century, as exemplified by articles such as those by Steffens. Clearly, if more people had access to a single writer, that writer's influence would expand. What the articles said is not the point to be stressed in this case—although complimentary to all candidates, Steffens seemed to favor La Follette, Debs, and Roosevelt, in that order—rather, what is significant is Steffens as an early example of a nationwide commentator and analyst serving in a role much like that of a modern television commentator. In that context, perhaps, his role and significance as a magazine reporter can most usefully be interpreted today.

Steffens's verbal reconstruction of "the System," was, so far, a structure made up of articles about cities at the base, with articles about states on the next level, followed on the third level by an exposure of federal corruption. Each of these levels was supported by various biographical and human interest articles, not to mention the support they gained from the work of other muckrakers. But the source from which corruption flowed down to the rest of "the System" was still to be analyzed.

Steffens pinpointed that source in "Tweed Days in St. Louis," his first article, and in every article after that. "The corruption of St. Louis," he wrote, "came from the top. The best citizens—the merchants and big financiers—used to rule the town, and they ruled it well."[9] Reformists would have to defeat business interests at the top levels if "the System" was to be cured. Steffens found bribe takers at every level of government, but the bribe giver had been, in every case, a businessman. Equal opportunity was an essential element in democratic government, and the desire to be given a better than equal chance with public funds drove businessmen to corrupting politicians, who were in control of public funds. Steffens noted in his *Autobiography:* "I had seen and written that what these big and little businesses all had in common was not size but need of privileges: franchises and special legislation, which required legislative corruption, protective tariffs, interpretations of laws in their special interest or leniency or 'protection' in the enforcement of laws, calling for 'pulls' with judges, prosecutors, and the police."[10]

Consequently, reform's biggest enemy—be it reform in politics, slum conditions, resource management, morals, or any of the other areas attacked by Steffens and his fellow muckrakers—was business; for business was the major motivating force in the country, at least in Steffens's eyes. The fight, to him, was between the people (or democracy) on the one side and business (or financial aristocracy) on the other. The reformer's problem, at base, was that businessmen were the most respected members of society. The right to rise on the economic (and social) ladder was the promise of America, and those who had done so were heroes, to be emulated and respected, not attacked. In claiming that these men were responsible for corruption Steffens was attacking the status quo in which most of his readers hoped to succeed. But the corrupt sought to stay at the top, and in doing so destroyed democracy by eliminating the equal opportunities that had allowed them to succeed and that would allow others to follow them. As Steffens claimed in italics in *The Struggle for Self-Government:*

Political corruption, then, is a force by which a representative democracy is transformed into an oligarchy representative of special interests, and the medium of the revolution is the party. Indeed, often the men leading reform had to break rank because they discovered they were attacking their own special privilege. [11]

Attempts to reform government served to show the typical citizen that it was his hero, the businessman, who had corrupted in the first place. The necessary ingredient for reform was a selfless devotion to democracy, and only the uniquely patriotic chose country over self.

As the above quotation indicates, one of the controls business had over people was politics. Having great wealth, it controlled the political parties by supporting the men and politics it wanted, using its wealth to defeat opposition. Thus, as his articles on cities, states, and the federal government had shown, every level had officials who were spoken of as "safe," or, even worse, as the representatives of certain business interests. Business controlled both parties, and public divergence of opinion was minute if compared to a fundamental uniformity within "the System." Voting Republican or Democratic was, for all realistic purposes, voting "Business."

After all, weren't most congressmen, governors, mayors, and city councilmen merely businessmen who had gone into politics? One of Steffens's articles, "Ohio, a Tale of Two Cities," told the story of why and how Mark Hanna had entered government service—for business reasons; and Hanna had been one of the most powerful men in the country. As historian Russel B. Nye has noted, after the 1896 election "Hanna was undisputed master of the Republican party and the nearest thing to a national political boss that politics had seen." [12]

Thus, business was the top block on the political pyramid; Steffens analyzed it in a series of articles published between

September 1910 and April 1911 in *Everybody's Magazine* under
the title, "It: An Exposition of the Sovereign Political Power of
Organized Business." Since his readers already knew that business controlled politics, and since other writers, including Ida
Tarbell at *McClure's,* had already delved quite deeply into business, Steffens changed his approach.

He analyzed business for reasons similar to those he had
analyzed government for—to see if the people could rule. Obviously business ruled government, he said so in the first article in the series: "In all quiet conflicts between our national
business organization and our national political organization,
business wins. That is to say, under normal conditions the
power of business is greater than our political power."[13] But
could anyone successfully reach the top in business and thus
have resultant political power? If business was democratic—if
everyone had the opportunity to become a success—then
democracy, in one rather distorted sense at least, still worked.
Steffens's real question, then, was whether the Horatio Alger
story fit existing conditions. Could anyone rise via business, or
was democracy as outdated in business as in politics?

His conclusion, briefly, was that an oligarchy even more advanced than the one controlling the nation controlled business. Second, he illustrated that Wall Street, or business on a
national scale, was essentially dominated by bankers, since they
controlled the credit that was essential to business. Finally, if
one man controlled the banks, he was the dictator of business
and, since business ruled politics, the ruler of the country.
And, Steffens claimed, his research revealed that banking had,
like politics, gone through a period of evolution over the last
few decades until finally one man, J. Pierpont Morgan,
reigned supreme.

It should be stressed that the type of democracy Steffens
had attempted to define was a far cry from the traditional
democracy that the majority of the reading public hoped
would be established by the Progressive movement. Steffens's
straining of the definition of democracy was a last-ditch effort
to prove that opportunity, at least in the business sense, still

existed. Success would have confirmed only a distant relation to traditional American democracy, at best. Business, after all, was not sacred in the Constitution. It held no particular place in the formula of democracy believed in America other than one that had evolved as the country grew. Steffens's conclusion that business was not democratic did not really clinch his argument against American politics; it merely reinforced something he had suspected long before he began any articles on business.

The entire moral code of the society was what Steffens really doubted. In much of his earlier muckraking, corruption was traced as far back as the Pennsylvania Railroad, which loomed above several states as the source of economic and thus political power; and yet, when questioned, a director of "the Penn" asked Steffens, "What do you want to pick on a little fellow like me for?"[14] In the most significant article of the series, "The Politics of Business," Steffens aired a dilemma that was increasingly a source of discomfort to him: "My study of business has so confused my sense of morals that I wouldn't dare to condemn Mr. Murphy or Matt Quay or Boss Cox [notorious political bosses]. Political vices are virtue in business. Bad politics is good business."[15]

This was written, take note, in 1910, when muckraking was in sharp decline, if not exhausted. Such doubt of the guilt of known political bosses would hardly have been thought let alone printed in a popular magazine five years earlier. Two factors in Steffens's background were influencing him greatly: his study of clinical psychology, which had taught him to look deeper than the individual for the causes of a problem, and a growing awareness that the men in on reform were the same men who were, innocently but intrinsically, in on "the System" of corruption.

"The System," as Steffens chose to call it, was complete. Several other muckrakers had done a great deal to fill in various proofs from other aspects of American society, but Steffens's work alone went far beyond what was essential to prove his premise. There are several implications in his analysis that should be considered.

First, "the System" was predictable—it was the same at every level and on every occasion. Reviewing a new charter aimed at reforming a city, Steffens wrote that "back of this charter and working through it, there were the same old boss, ring, and machine, governing Philadelphia as St. Louis, Minneapolis, New York, and Pittsburgh were governed."[16] This factor about Steffens's work most impresses historian Louis Filler:

> Steffens was accounted political muckraking's greatest authority because he gave more than sensations, more than corruption: he gave the *formula* for municipal corruption as it was to be found not only in St. Louis, or Minneapolis, or elsewhere, but *anywhere*. With the laboratory scientist's eye for fundamentals he traced out the American city structure with the party machine acting between organized business, the official city government, graft circles and plain criminals.[17]

Indeed, so complete was Steffens's picture of the form of corruption that he once drew a chart of it in front of an audience and had them, when he was completed, yell out the names of the local businessmen and politicians and where they belonged on the chart.[18]

Second, and following logically, "the form of government did not matter; . . .constitutions and charters did not affect essentially the actual government."[19] This, of course, implied that "the System" was an organic development rather than an artificial order placed on society by written documents. The implications of this factor are staggering, for if one accepts it he must also grant that the job of reforming government is vastly more difficult than it had previously appeared. New types of city government, new constitutions, and such innovations were beside the point. Theoretically, any new form of government was doomed in advance. Consequently, planning new forms of rule without consideration of the motivations and nature of the people to be governed and the particular situations involved was a wasted effort.

Third, and directly related, was the nature of American

priorities. In *The Shame of the Cities* Steffens wrote that "the boss is not a political, he is an American institution," and that "the spirit of graft and lawlessness is the American spirit."[20] The full implications of these statements, which will be discussed later, were to be found in the extent that reform failed or succeeded. One of the products of the reform movement was experimentation with the organization of government, especially at the local level with the institution of the strong city manager; but, if Steffens was right, city government organizations were aiming at the wrong target when they attempted to solve their problems by changing the format of the government rather than the nature of the governed. The tragedy of what Steffens exposed was not the weakness of the American governmental system, it was the weakness of the American people.

Finally, and most obviously, the biggest power in "the System" was business, or, in the philosophic sense, capitalism. If the proof was truly in the pudding, it was obvious that the American public was willing to sell its democratic heritage and interests for (or to) its business interests. The great and abiding conclusion, to express it in one of the scores of ways Steffens put it, was that "financial power is not merely financial, it is political. It is a matter of the management of the men."[21] With this conclusion, the path Steffens followed for the rest of his life seems perfectly understandable.

The Context of Muckraking

Steffens's success as a muckraker, indeed the success of the muckrakers in general, was based on a direct appeal to the moral and civic pride of the mass middle class rather than on any intellectual challenge. With a few notable exceptions, the exposé journalists of the Progressive era scrupulously avoided even the suggestion of any radical changes in the basic arrangement of society. Rather, they emphasized the need for a rejuvenation of traditional Protestant values. From one point of view the muckrakers insisted that the government had changed too much, that what was needed was a return to solid old virtues rather than radical new theories. In the dedication of *The Struggle for Self-Government* to the Czar of Russia, Steffens wrote:

Your majesty should know that after our first, the bloody American revolution, a second, bloodless, nameless and slow, set in. After we had established "government of the people, by the people, and for the people," we went back to work. We let who would rule us, and somehow or other it has happened that those men have come into power who see in government,—what Kings see, Sire,—a source, not of common equal justice for all, but of special advantages for the few.[22]

The appeal of exposure, therefore, rested on a call for action and civic responsibility—a sort of fundamentalist political revival—and not on any innovative or radical plea for change. The introduction to *The Shame of the Cities* assures readers that "good conduct in the individual, simple honesty, courage, and efficiency . . . would result in a revolution, more radical and terrible to existing institutions from Congress to the Church, from the bank to the ward organization, than socialism or even anarchy."[23] Couched between the lines of much of Steffens's public writing is the implication that the inevitable result of continuous inaction would be far more radical and devastating than the current bad state of affairs. If socialism or anarchy were to be avoided, he warned (at least in the early part of the muckraking period), immediate public action was necessary. The dedication of *The Struggle for Self-Government* to the Czar clearly implied that kings had nothing to fear from democracy as it was operating in the United States.

"The more the muckrakers acquainted the Protestant Yankee with what was going on around him," Richard Hofstadter has claimed, "the more guilty and troubled he felt."[24] Responsibility for the corruption being reported was placed squarely on the shoulders of the public. In 1906 Steffens wrote a newspaper analysis of the federal government, in which he claimed:

My belief is that so far as our Government is bad the evil thereof is traceable, not to particular bad men, but to the good citizen; and not alone to their neglect, but their (often unconscious) participation in some form of (often unidentified) graft, keeps them "apathetic." Bankers call themselves good citizens; I know three or four who are. I should like to have the others ask themselves why they are leaving reform to what they call "Socialists." Isn't it because they are not only busy, but in on the graft somewhere?[25]

Another historian, Lloyd Morris, has noted that "Steffens was trying to drive home to the American people ... their own moral complicity. It was only by their tacit consent that representative government had ceased to represent them."[26]

But, while the muckrakers acquired considerable fame from slapping the American public on the wrist for its moral laxity, they dared not offend that public by suggesting that there was anything fundamentally wrong with the basic form of government. Being bawled out by the muckrakers made readers feel that they had, in part at least, paid for their shortcomings, much as a bad child feels after a spanking. But the average reader, as was implied by Steffens, had far too much invested in the corruption to want any drastic alteration of the social, political, or economic system that had evolved in that "second, bloodless" revolution.

As the muckraking movement progressed and Steffens observed more and more unconscious graft among those who should have supported reform, he personally grew skeptical of the faith the common man placed in the fundamental quality of the existing social and economic system. Comparison of the path he followed and the paths followed by most of his fellow muckrakers, who became apologists for business, indicates that Steffens was at base more liberal and, it should be stressed, more scientific in his search for a solution to corruption than the majority of the muckrakers. Of his reformer compatriots he wrote, "It was amazing to me to hear how little the muckrakers had learned from their muckraking. ... They were thoughtless conservatives, as undisturbed as the conservatives they despised."[27] When other Progressives felt reform had gone far enough, Steffens parted company from them and continued to question the status quo. At least one of the reasons for his leaving *McClure's* was S. S. McClure's editing and rewriting of his articles so as not to offend the general reading public by their radical content. Steffens was saying things McClure felt would deviate drastically from popular opinion—and McClure had almost a sixth sense of public taste.

Steffens himself came to believe that the American public was brainwashed; he credited his German education with saving him from oversimplifying the problems of politics as the general public had. They believed that good men and old-time morality would make everything better; Steffens, on the other hand, often felt these to be a major source rather than the cure for corrupt government. "Quick, superficial, common-sense convictions were apt to be nothing but protective guards set up by the poor weak human mind to save itself from the temptation and effort to think. . . ."[28] Steffens had to keep such beliefs out of his articles, however. He was expected to reinforce what the public, and S. S. McClure, believed. Thus, in 1906, for this and a variety of other reasons, Steffens, with several other former *McClure's* writers each having their own motives for departure, bought out the *American Magazine*. Steffens soon sold his share of that venture, feeling the pressure of his own investment working to undermine his freedom to criticize. He found that even he, when he had a vested interest in magazine profits and losses, could be tempted to hedge in his analysis. He therefore sold out immediately, not allowing his own money to corrupt him.

Steffens's letters and *Autobiography* for this era illustrate that he was personally becoming far more radical than his public writings indicated. For one thing, investigation had shown him that many of the reformers were naïvely simplistic in their faith in the essential democratic and middle-class nature of the electorate, while the bosses he attacked were often intellectually honest and competent administrators far more capable of handling the complex problems of emerging government in a humanitarian, if not legal and scrupulously efficient, manner.

In a letter to an Indianapolis reformer seeking aid, Steffens wrote: "Oh, you Business Men, with your business reforms! You will ruin yourselves yet. I laugh, but I could weep. Don't you know that back of the petty larceny there is grand larceny, and that back of the political corruption, and supporting it, is business corruption."[29] Businessmen, who were heroes to most reformers (who suggested that the best government was one run by someone who had been a proven success in business), disenchanted Steffens. Very few of the businessmen reformers were willing, he felt, to give up the profit motive. While they might do so unknowingly, they maintained the theory that what profited them also profited the country.

In 1908, Theodore Roosevelt sent a letter to Steffens in which he stated that "what [was] needed [was] the *fundamental fight for morality,*" and he underscored the last four words. Roosevelt added in a postscript that socialism wouldn't work. Steffens replied that "we may have to go" as far as socialism. "If we do, to get things right, then I, for one, should be willing to go there." He further suggested that a fight for morality would have less chance for success than "abolishing in some way the *greater* privileges granted by government."[30] He pointed toward public ownership, and that seemed far too radical for either Roosevelt or the public in general.

Also, while the businessmen Steffens observed were generally naïve, the corrupt politicians he knew were both knowledgeable and competent. They corrupted cities because they had been trained by their environment to do so. The men themselves, Steffens thought, were not to blame, "it was privilege that had to be dealt with, not men. . . . To throw out the rascals and put into office honest men without removing that which makes good men do bad things was as irrational as our experience had taught us it was 'unpractical.' "[31] That was why reform never lasted—it never cured any of the causes of the sickness of the body politic; and that is also why Steffens grew to feel that a fundamental change in the order of society was necessary. The reformers claimed to be honest, not knowing that their training had dulled their sense of honesty, at least in Steffens's eyes. His training in clinical psychology had taught him to distrust those who thought they knew what was best. But, Steffens continued, the corrupted, who were intellectually honest with themselves,

know that they are sinners and they don't deny it (except under oath), and they don't try to justify themselves. That is why it is such a comfort to sit down and talk with them. They accept, and you can start with, the facts, as you can in a conversation with scientists. They can be saved, and some day, when they are asked to they may help us to save society. They are our best men. . . . But the petty honest men who do not know that or when or how they sin, they will not face and so cannot deal with things as they are.[32]

Clinical psychology had conditioned him to be more prone to accept scientific method than good intentions as a source of effective reform. To his friend Brand Whitlock he wrote of "the acknowledged grafter. They are really interesting people. They're interesting for their honesty."[33] In 1908, he wrote his sister, "I know things are all wrong somehow; and fundamentally; but I don't know what the matter is and I don't know *what* to do about it." Later in the letter he concluded, "I am socialistic, but I'm not yet a Socialist."[34]

This type of thinking was far from the mainstream. Steffens found that, as he saw it, the truth was that the people were basically incapable of believing in either their complicity or, subconsciously, in the practicability of actual democracy. Whatever, he was moving toward the political left. Eugene V. Debs, running for President on the Socialist ticket in 1908, wrote to Steffens, "You have written from and have been inspired by a social brain, a social heart and a social conscience and if you are not a socialist I do not know one."[35]

And yet, while he had many points of philosophy that seemed to come directly from socialism, there were some basic fundamental differences about his liberalism and Debs's that should be clarified. Like Woodrow Wilson, but unlike Teddy Roosevelt, Steffens disliked any concentration of power, be it public or private. Socialism would create a federal bureaucracy that would be just as stifling to individual freedom as monopolies had been, or at least it seemed so to Steffens. While public ownership might be better than private ownership, the new "System" that would be necessary to facilitate such an arrangement would be larger and more powerful than ever. As historian David Chalmers has concluded about Steffens, "The two aspects [about socialism] which held him back were a rather vague dislike of concentrated economic power and his strong opposition to the idea of class struggle. He could not bear to see the centralization of power in industry and finance that the Socialists believed was involved in the transition from monopoly to government ownership."[36]

Further, the very concept of a "System" implied that corruption was institutionalized and that a change in the institution was essential to lasting reform. Of course, the reading public remembered Steffens's articles for the corruption and specific names, dates, and facts they revealed, not for the theoretical implications of those details. The American public had little patience with theories, and the common cry that immorality bred corruption was far easier to accept than complex or radical social theories.

But to Steffens the tragic implications of "the System," as noted earlier, demanded attention. Reform, to be successful, had to defeat "the System." He had discovered that political organization sprang from the society, not from any documents. "The paper government," he felt, "did not count."[37] Everywhere he went he found that the men responsible for corruption were, quite naïvely, claiming credit for the local reform movement; and he found that the men publicly condemned as corrupt were, in fact, more intellectually honest. If reform was to come about, society itself had to be drastically altered.

As it was, people couldn't even help their own inclinations. Our system of government established "the ideal of success, [and] set up temptations of power and riches to men and nations—if they were brave enough to risk and able enough to escape the threats and penalties for getting caught. These warnings keep off all but the best men, biologically best. Then when these best men succeed we honor them, and if they slip we hate and punish them. What we ought to do is let the losers of the race go, and take down the prizes we offer to the winner."[38] To take down the prizes, of course, meant a complete revamping of the economic system that, in one sense, most of the reformers had set out to maintain.

Steffens had in his student days set out in search of a foundation for ethics, and he had not abandoned his search. The American reform movement, on the other hand, had set out to cure the ailments of free enterprise that had emerged as urbanization and industrialization had infected it in the late nineteenth century. They were different goals that had, for a while, followed the same path. But Steffens was following a different drummer and, since he had not yet answered his question, was eagerly awaiting the next liberal cause. The society at large, however, was satisfied by the limited change that had occurred.

The Application of Power

Although Steffens's power and fame were fleeting, they were substantial while they lasted. He was preeminent among the muckrakers. The meaning of such a distinction deserves attention.

By 1903, Steffens was well enough known to have a cigar named after him, a dubious distinction but certainly an indication of wide popularity. His reputation, however, was clearly something separate from his personality. When Ohio reformer Frederic Howe first met the young journalist face to face he had trouble believing his eyes; "I pictured him big, blond, and fierce," he wrote, "a militant reformer, hating corruption. The man who appeared had soft eyes and a quiet voice. . . . I thought there must be some mistake—my visitor must be someone else."[39]

And yet, if his appearance seemed unique to fellow reformers, it must have seemed just as unique to the corrupt, whom Steffens usually sincerely liked. While they feared him, they also were fascinated by a man who was so interested in their side of the story. Once Steffens had established himself with a local boss, that boss would often ask Steffens to return again—for a long chat. The bosses seemed to be fascinated by the picture Steffens painted of them, even though they were also threatened by it. When he approached "Iz" Durham, the boss of Philadelphia, for example, Durham cut him off before he had a chance to say anything. "I want to ask you a couple of questions," Durham began, and soon it was unclear who was interviewing whom.[40]

The reason for Steffens's interest, no doubt, was the fact that the bosses themselves were not aware—at least in a moral and philosophical sense—what the implications of their acts were. Durham was sincerely interested in what he considered good government, and he ran his city with that intent. When he finally met a reformer who would listen calmly to his side of the story, and not spout theory as if it had heavenly sanction, he was anxious to find out what he did that that individual thought was so wrong. Steffens was just the man; he was the last man to place guilt, especially on the usually accused. Durham acted on a day-to-day basis, like most people in most jobs, handling each situation as best he could; he lacked the overall picture necessary to total understanding. Steffens, also unsure about that same philosophy, was always eager to talk with such experienced men. While other reformers seemed to forget that they were usually themselves unexperienced in the day-to-day practice of government, Steffens realized that bosses were experienced and capable administrators, to an extent that would shame many reformers. So Steffens never appeared as an enemy to the men he attacked, except in the public sense. Privately they liked him; he was an honest man doing his job, just as they saw themselves; he was not a hypocritical businessman nor a politically naïve reformer.

This does not mean that the bosses underrated his power; in fact, they probably respected it more because they knew it was deserved. But they did not forget that he was out to expose them. When Steffens tried to interview the boss of Rhode Island, a blind old man named Charles R. Brayton, Brayton's relatives refused to allow him an interview. While Steffens credited this to the family's fear of the old man's candor, the same family had allowed an interview with reporters from both the *New York Evening Post* and the *Springfield Republican*. It was Steffens's power they feared, not the old man's candor.[41]

Steffens's power is also clear when seen in the context of the people he helped. The aid he gave Governor La Follette in Wisconsin is a good example. La Follette's wife recalled in her biography of her husband that "it had become a subconscious prayer" with her that Steffens would lend support to her husband. "I was confident," she continued, that "he had the ability and insight to get at the truth in spite of the maze of lies he would encounter."[42] (She was right.) When Steffens first arrived, La Follette was under heavy attack, considered a radical at home, and unknown nationally. He had suffered from smears by the Stalwart local press, and even Steffens originally approached him as a demagogue, having heard nothing but bad about him.

But La Follette won Steffens's support, and issues of *McClure's* were sold out immediately in Wisconsin and all the surrounding states. The opposition press argued that Steffens had been bought, or that he had been duped by the governor, but such accusations were obvious attempts at saving face, since they came from the same papers that had previously welcomed Steffens, who they supposed would expose La Follette.

Beyond having a strong local influence on La Follette's career, Steffens's attention caused several other major magazines to turn their attention to Wisconsin; *Collier's Weekly*, *Harper's Weekly*, *Outlook*, and *Review of Reviews*, to mention a few, soon turned out articles praising "Fighting Bob, The Little Giant."[43] For years to come La Follette would gain support from Steffens. In fact, when he started his own magazine, his

lead article in the first issue, "The Mind of a State," was written, by special request, by Lincoln Steffens.

At the height of his power Steffens was recognized as capable of influencing national politics to a measurable degree. At
one time Theodore Roosevelt went so far as to attempt to gain
Steffens's help in achieving his goals (which, it should be
noted, Steffens did not always agree with). In the fall of 1903
Roosevelt invited both Steffens and S.S. McClure to the White
House, where he suggested that Steffens do a series on the
various fights he was having with labor and business. Fortu-
nately, since it would have compromised Steffens's honesty to
work under the direction of a particular politician and since
Steffens's special area was government corruption and not
labor or business legislation, the idea was soon dismissed. But
McClure realized the implications of the request perfectly well
when he said, "I believe we can do more toward making a
President of the United States than any other twenty
organs."[44] A bit conceited perhaps, but not far from true.

While Steffens's popularity with the reading public declined
rather quickly, many of the people he had known remained in
politics for years to come. With them he was still considered a
thoughtful and knowledgeable analyst, and so his influence
remained longer than his popularity. Speaking of the years
immediately preceding World War I, when most people had
either forgotten Steffens or rejected him as a radical, historian
Henry F. May ranks Steffens as something of an eminent figure, a go-between for the socially and politically disenfran-
chised radicals and the political power structure, saying that
"Steffens was a far more powerful figure than the outside
radicals of the far left."[45]

Boston

Steffens had spent eight years establishing himself as one of
the most knowledgeable men in the country on the subject of
governmental reform. His opinions on the subject were widely

known, highly respected, and greatly feared in certain circles. But in 1908 he had never actively attempted to lead a city toward a better tomorrow. In the fall of that year he moved to Boston, where he was to attempt to do exactly that.

Early in the year Mr. Edward A. Filene, a wealthy Boston merchant who had embraced the liberal movement, told Steffens that he would support a year-long study of Boston if it led to some concrete proposals for the city's betterment. Increasingly disenchanted with what he saw as the failure of others to effect change, Steffens accepted, leaving his home in Connecticut for one in Boston in October. He was to spend close to a year there and would, in general, accomplish nothing.

Boston was to be tackled on a much larger scale than anything Steffens had previously attempted, even in writing. There were to be two books, one describing the state of government and one making a plan for the reform of the city. The plan Steffens devised for the reform of Boston was to be initiated immediately and completed by 1915, a date he had been forced to compromise on when the men involved in the scheme protested that 1922, the date Steffens wanted, was "too visionary."

The crux of Steffens's plan developed from a concept he evolved from observing the political boss of Boston, Martin Lomasny. Working on the theory that "good citizens" had always failed in reform because of their complicity in the corruption, self-deception, and moral weakness, Steffens wanted to "give up the good men and try the strong men." The bosses were honest with themselves, never attempting to hide under a pose of respectability. They were also successful in whatever they tried, an American virtue that Steffens—a pragmatist —respected and commented upon:

It was true that the strong men were often bad men or busy with bad business, but, I argued, if we could start these natural leaders to working on our good plan, they might become interested in it. They would find it big and difficult, but they liked hard, large jobs. There would be obstacles and opposition, but they loved a fight. Indeed, it was the fighting which might convert these bad men to carry on where good men commonly lay down.[46]

Lomasny gave Steffens a new view on the reasoning behind the existence of the boss. " 'I think,' " he told Steffens, " 'that there's got to be in every ward somebody that any bloke can come to—no matter what he's done—and get help. Help, you understand; none of your law and your justice, but help.' "[47]

The logic of this statement appeared to Steffens as totally Christian, and exactly what the city needed. Using Lomasny's statement as a basis, he suggested that a committee—made up of a lawyer, a businessman, a minister, and Lomasny, a boss and Christian—be established to deal with the problems of Boston's citizens in such a way that the committee would be a service rather than a threat to criminals. A second and more traditional objective taken on by the committee was the coordination of the various plans for civic improvement that were proposed by various groups, in the hope that a clearing committee would eliminate duplication, graft, and high expense.

The failure of the plan can be traced, of course, to the failure of the citizens to abandon their individual goals for the sake of the public good. While the members of the committee remained Christian, the forces that played on them and around them refused to follow their lead. Power seemed to return to its old location; the strong men on the committee became, in a sense, bosses. Just as there had been bosses before, there were bosses again. The problem can be traced to a single American trait: "Our ideal," Steffens concluded, "is individual, not social, success, and that's what has to be changed, this ideal."[48]

Intrinsic in Steffens's concept of "the System" was the notion that the actual form of government would reflect the nature of the people it governed. The Boston 1915 Plan was Steffens's attempt to change things on paper; but he, of all people, should have known that it did not really matter what the government on paper said. "The System," being a natural phenomenon, did not mold to the artificial systems man attempted to impose.

Steffens was essentially out of his element in the Boston ex-periment. He was not a natural leader or planner; rather, he was a first-rate reporter and a lower-echelon social philosopher, using the implications of what he reported as the foundation of his philosophy. His attempt at political planning in an administrative post called for abilities he simply did not possess, a fact he realized soon after leaving Boston. Intellec-tuals were fine in the realm of theory, but action required the firm and sure grasp of a man—perfectly content with his beliefs—who was able to act without hesitation. Steffens, while always an independent and liberal thinker, was never sure that his opinions would remain the same—in fact, he was almost certain that they wouldn't—and was thus reticent to impose them upon others in terms of concrete actions.

Steffens also failed because he was tired of muckraking. Walter Lippman, his assistant during the year he was in Bos-ton, had to write the chapter on Boston's scandals. "I had re-ported the like so often," Steffens recalled, "that my mind or my stomach revolted at the repetition. Boston was so like other cities that I could not—I did not—muckrake its politics, which were all business."[49] Had he attempted the Boston 1915 Plan five years earlier, there can be little doubt that he would have gone about it differently and would have achieved al-tered, though not necessarily more successful, results.

Steffens's distaste for repeated scandal reflected a similar distaste on the public's part. Change took place gradually, but the public was tired of reform as much as Steffens was. For numerous reasons, including a sincere distaste for being con-stantly attacked for their own moral laxity, the reading public no longer wanted to be told that they were guilty and corrupt. They led what they thought of as honest lives, and as criticism grew stronger and critics became repetitious, they simply started to ignore reform. Whatever the reason, neither of the Boston books was ever published, and all the public ever saw of the research was a few articles in magazines.

CHAPTER 5

Radical

The McNamara Case

W ITHIN a month after accepting a position on the *New York Globe,* a descendant of the old *Commercial Advertiser,* in the autumn of 1911, Steffens organized a syndicate of several papers to run articles, written by him, covering the bombing of the *Los Angeles Times* building and the trial of the two men, the McNamara brothers, thought to be responsible for it and the resultant deaths of twenty-one men. The McNamaras' attorneys, headed by Steffens's friend Clarence Darrow, felt that the case was close to hopeless. Evidence was strong against the two, and Darrow was worried (quite literally) sick that they would hang.

Steffens believed the two men guilty, but felt that their guilt was beside the point. The important thing, he insisted, was that the public understand the reasons behind the bombing and that some progress be gained from the whole ordeal. After all, people didn't bomb buildings for small reasons. "It is a social manifestation of a condition, not a mere legal offense, this crime," Steffens told the judge presiding in the case.[1] And so Steffens undertook to do what the judge could not do; he tried to see if he could make the case the beginning of a new order of bloodless Los Angeles (and American) business-labor relations.

His intention, then, was to get a confession from the McNamaras (on the condition that all charges against them be dropped), explain the cause of the bombing so "that anybody, even an employer of labor, can comprehend it," and use the new information as a source of understanding labor's point of view.[2] To accomplish this end he enlisted the aid of news-paperman E. W. Scripps, the liberal head of a chain of liberal papers, Clarence Darrow, and a group of influential businessmen from Los Angeles, headed by General Otis, owner of the bombed *Times,* and his business manager and son-in-law, Harry Chandler.

In order to gain business support, Steffens asked several business leaders to consider the advantages of a peaceful rather than a vengeful conclusion. What he said to General Otis is, essentially, what he said to all the businessmen he approached:

This is a proposition to stop a fight, a fool fight, and try another, better way to settle a difference. How do you stop a fight? By stopping the fellow who has just been struck from striking the next blow. In this fight it is capital's turn. Labor hit you hard, with dynamite, fire, killings. And now you've got labor down where you can give it some legal dynamite and a bit of legal murder. What would happen if, now, you, the *Times* that was blown up, and Los Angeles, should say "No. No hangings, no force, no wrongs. We'll not only let your agents go; we will sit down with your picked labor representatives, and we'll see together if we can't do something no city has ever done, plan together for the highest-paid, most productive labor and management in the world?"[3]

Although he never said so to anyone directly involved at the time, Steffens was attempting to go around the old "System," and, as he said often, start a new one based on application of the Golden Rule to a modern problem and see if he could be successful.

Surprisingly, things went quite well for a while. Darrow agreed, the business element agreed, and even the two men on trial agreed. While total pardon was impossible, the McNamaras finally said they would be willing to accept a life sentence for James B. McNamara, who acted as an individual, and a shorter sentence for John J. McNamara, who was the secretary of the Structural Iron Workers and thus was taken to represent organized labor. They demanded that there be a conference of labor and business and that others being sought in connection with the case be pardoned. The case would hurt Darrow's prestige with labor, of course, because such a conclusion would imply labor's guilt in general; but Darrow was willing to suffer the consequences, especially when he found that his clients were in favor of it and when he considered the chances for a better conclusion.

Then, however, things started going awry. First, Darrow was accused of attempting to bribe one of the jurors. Second, the Erector's Association—an organization representing business—raised fifteen thousand dollars to help convict the two laborers. Since the association, not Los Angeles based, was not accessible to Steffens, he could not give it his persuasive arguments. Third, the churches reacted to the decision rendered before the judge passed sentence, and resultant changes in public opinion forced the judge to deal a harsh public condemnation, ruining any chance for progress from lessons learned. This third reason—the one Steffens most lamented—proved to him that the Christian churches were not Christian. "What they preached was hate and disappointed revenge," he wrote in his *Autobiography*. [4]

For the rest of his life Steffens wore a small gold cross from his watch chain, calling himself "the only Christian on earth." One of his friends, Mabel Dodge, described the effect of the tragedy on Steffens and the rest of the liberals involved:

Clarence Darrow, even then the biggest criminal lawyer in America, cried in court and Steff bought that gold cross and put it on as a kind of badge of failure. . . . Steff couldn't get over it. He started to work for their pardons. So Steff was always interviewing governors. Sometimes he was almost successful. His friends got used to Steff's journeys off to interview governors. . . . [He] was always reporting to [the McNamaras] his hopes, his failures. Finally, I believe one of them sent him word to give up, let it go. But Steff couldn't. By his personal influence he had put them there; by the same he must get them released. But he never succeeded. [5]

The only effect the case had beyond embittering Steffens even more toward "the System" was to place his name back into the headlines. He continued to write his account of the case and its implications for three months after the judge's decision was handed down, and Darrow's trial for jury tampering dragged on for several months more. To his sisters Steffens wrote, "It was a hopeless sort of a job, and very nerveracking in its difficulties and disappointments."[6] It was late summer before the ordeal ended. As a result of it he had a lengthy spell of depression bordering on illness. His appeals continued endlessly. John McNamara did manage to get paroled eleven years later, but his brother Jim died in Folsom Prison in 1941, after Steffens's own death. In her autobiography, Steffens's second wife finishes his story. In San Quentin he had "befriended young lost boys who came in angry and truculent, and fought for justice inside the prison. For years men came out of San Quentin telling what J. B. had done for them; they almost worshipped him.... [Later] he had been sent to Folsom, a harsher jail, a punishment for helping other prisoners, and he had also been deprived of his few comforts—slippers, books (including Steffens's *Autobiography)*, and a strip of carpet he had used for more than a decade."[7] Such was exactly the type of thing Steffens had hoped to cure, and such was the cause of his statement that he was "the only Christian on earth." But, while he considered his attempt an unqualified failure, it did most likely save both the McNamaras from death penalties.

It also serves to illustrate the gap growing between labor and management in these years. Steffens's "System" had, at long last, separated the nation into two distinct groups —workers and capitalists—and the consequences involved in the McNamara case probably did more than any other single thing to force Steffens toward revolutionary action. He became acutely aware of the existence of classes in the United States; and soon he would be preaching the end of a class system. Indeed, nothing so prepared him to be receptive to communism as did his experience with reactionary capitalists, as best illustrated by the men who had gone back on their words in the McNamara case.

No longer was Steffens a liberal. He had seen too much.

The McNamara case had set the stage, Greenwich Village was to teach the theory, and soon revolution would trigger the response.

The Greenwich Village Intellectuals

Sitting one autumn afternoon in 1912 in the plush parlor of Mabel Dodge's all white apartment at 23 Fifth Avenue, Steffens suggested to his hostess that she sponsor weekly evenings for the sake of good conversation. She agreed. A complex and fascinating character, Mabel Dodge soon became a centripetal force pulling most of New York's radicals, artists, authors, travelers, intellectuals, and liberals into her salon, which became famous as a center of free speech and innovative radical thought.

A wealthy socialite divorcée, Mabel Dodge had an insatiable desire to be in the midst of everything. A friend, journalist Hutchins Hapgood, recalled her as "the only woman I know who might fairly be called 'God-drunk.' If at any time she became aware of something lying just out of reach, she was intensely restless until she had drawn it into her web. She was always talking about 'It'; ... the unseen cause of all seen things, ... the Infinite."[8] Steffens told her that she had the perfect "centralizing, magnetic, social faculty" to make such evenings a success, and he was right.[9]

It is in the context of such a company that Steffens must be considered in the early teens of this century, a period historian Henry F. May has perceptively labeled "the end of American innocence." The last remnant of his progressivism was being destroyed in California. Incapable of sustained pessimism, Steffens instinctively joined a group of men and women, mostly younger than himself, in seeking a new cause. Anything radical was fair game, and discussion ranged from Socialists to psychology to art to anarchism. According to Mabel Dodge,

Socialists, Trade-Unionists, Anarchists, Suffragists, Poets, Relations
Lawyers, Murderers, "Old Friends." Psychoanalysts, I.W.W.'s, Single
Taxers, Birth Controlists, Newspapermen, Artists, Modern-Artists,
Clubwomen, Women's-place-is-in-the-home Women, Clergymen, and
just plain men all met there and, stammering in an unaccustomed
freedom a kind of speech called Free, exchanged a variousness in
vocabulary called, in euphemistic optimism, Opinions![10]

Despite the length of her list, other descriptions add
categories she omits. As her reputation and the reputation of
her evenings grew, the fare for discussion grew also. Eventually things got out of hand, but for a brief while her sparkling,
elegant salon boasted a circle of intellectuals that could vie
safely with Johnson's literary club or Emerson's restrained
Boston dinners.

An edited list of her guests would include woman's
liberationist Margaret Sanger; journalists Carl Hovey, Norman
and Hutchins Hapgood, and John Collier; journalist–social critics Walter Lippman and John Reed (and Steffens); literary
men like Carl Van Vechten, Floyd Dell, and Max Eastman;
Communists and Socialists like Bill Haywood, Emma Goldman, and English Wallings; artists like Maurice Becker and
Alfred Stieglitz; ex-reformers like Amos Pinchot and Fred and
Marie Howe; and poets like Edwin Arlington Robinson,
George Sylvester Viereck, and Amy Lowell; and that merely
tells the surface story. A more eclectic group of radicals has
never existed.

Steffens himself, hoping to recapture something akin to the
spirit he had felt as a student in Europe, moved to 42
Washington Square, in the heart of Greenwich Village, where
he shared a dilapidated old house with Jack Reed and some of
his classmates from Harvard college days. Reed was a West-
erner, the son of a reformer friend of Steffens, who had
gone to Harvard and, like his classmate Walter Lippman, had
been launched on an important literary career by Steffens.
Working for *Everybody's* in 1910, Steffens suggested an ap-
prentice system for developing young talent and, as a result,
recruited Lippman from the graduating class at Harvard as a

personal secretary. For Jack Reed, Steffens secured a position at the *American Magazine*.

Early in 1911 Steffens's wife died of Bright's disease. She was soon followed by his mother and father. If one were to determine the turning points in life by personal events, as no doubt one must, 1911 was a pivotal year. Muckraking and reform were dead, and so were the personal ties that could have held Steffens to the dead past. In the period following his return from Boston, Steffens and his wife had gradually drifted into New York's new intellectual bohemia. When Josephine died it was to this group Steffens turned to regain his bearings. Unlike the businessmen-reformers he had known, this new group was college-trained, artistic, sensitive, and markedly more bohemian. They were more cynical in their liberalism and more experimental in their vision. Steffens, aged forty-five, learned much from them, since they were unencumbered by many of the nineteenth-century blinders that had hindered their parents, the men of Steffens's age.

In fact, for seeking new solutions to old problems, he could not have turned to a better group, nor could he have gone to a better place. Greenwich Village contained the proper combination of men, freedom, and ideas to give new life and direction to his past studies. His day could include meetings with anyone from Theodore Dreiser or Sinclair Lewis to uptown politicos. It was one of those fortuitous combinations of men, times, and circumstances, and it saved Steffens from becoming a tradition-bound business liberal, as many of his former associates had.

But for Steffens as for his new friends, Greenwich Village was more of a rest stop on a journey than it was a final home. The men and women there were looking, and when they saw what promised to be more permanent intellectual homes, they moved on. Some of them never did find a home. Free-thinking and worldly innocents (if such a thing is possible), they were troubadours, listening to each other's stories and then going their separate ways. Something of their troubadour camaraderie is evident in the first stanza of a poem by the idealistic Jack Reed, the first in a small volume. The poem was titled as follows:

DEDICATORY
TO
LINCOLN STEFFENS,
ONE OF US;
THE ONLY MAN
WHO UNDERSTANDS MY ARGUMENTS

and the first stanza reads:

> STEFFENS, I hope I am doing no wrong to you
> By dedicating this doggerel song to you;
> Perhaps you'll resent
> The implied compliment,
> But light-hearted Liberty seems to belong to you.[11]

John Reed was later to follow Steffens to Russia, where he fell romantically in love with the revolution. He would produce there a memorable book about the revolution entitled *Ten Days that Shook the World.* But in those earlier days he was the embodiment of a free spirit, and Steffens guarded him almost as a son. A few years later, in 1920, when Reed died of typhus in Moscow and was buried in the Soviet Union, Steffens recalled him in a moving eulogy that was published in the *Freeman:*

When John Reed came, big and growing, handsome outside and beautiful inside, when that boy came down from Cambridge to New York, it seemed to me that I had never seen anything so near to pure joy. No ray of sunshine, no drop of foam, no young animal, bird, or fish, and no star was as happy. . . . If only we could keep him so, we might have a poet at last who would see and sing nothing but joy. Convictions were what I was afraid of. I tried to steer him away from convictions, that he might play with life; and see it all, love it all, live it all; tell it all; that he might be it all; but all, not any one thing. . . . Great days they were, or rather nights, when the boy would bang home late and wake me up to tell me what he had been and seen that day; the most wonderful thing in the world. Yes. Each night he had been and seen the most wonderful thing in the world.[12]

Reed was but one of the people into whom Steffens looked with hopes of finding himself. In Walter Lippman, and in countless other searching minds, Steffens was to continue to relive his own joys of discovery, keeping him young until death.

Steffens traveled throughout the few years between his wife's death and his interest in the Mexican Revolution, and his journeys were but indications of his restlessness, his desire to find a cause. He grasped at causes in hope of finding a new direction in which to channel his energy. His Boston book dragged on, more of a burden than a challenge. His personal life was chaotic; although he attracted many women, including one whom he was attracted to, he was ill at ease. Progressivism no longer gave him any satisfaction, and attendance at sessions about psychoanalysis at Mabel Dodge's salon no doubt caused him to doubt the value of his earlier conclusions. Freud and Jung replaced Wundt as his master of psychology. "I remember thinking how absurd had been my muckraker's descriptions of bad men and good men and the assumption that showing people facts and conditions would persuade them to alter them or their own conduct," he wrote of the effect of the new psychology.[13]

But these new insights caused new problems. Steffens found it harder and harder to write. To his sister he wrote, "I have friends of my age to whom the same thing has happened and to the writers among them in the same way. It is something like the change of life in women, and some of us speak of it in that phrase. What it is I don't know."[14] Steffens missed having a cause, and he missed feeling needed. As soon as he found Mexico, his hesitation and his problem disappeared.

CHAPTER 6

Revolutionary

The Mexican Revolution

BY the time World War I began, Steffens, who was in Italy, was convinced that "the revolution"—the one that would change the social order of the Western world—was at hand. The war in Europe was but the opening gun, he assumed, the political primer that would start a larger movement. So as to understand the powers he anticipated, he left Italy for Mexico, where "the revolution," on a small scale and in full progress, was easier to observe.

Mexico, long suffering under economic and political domination by larger capitalistic countries, was undergoing a series of political upheavals. Porfirio Diaz, President of Mexico, who had been a puppet of foreign investors, had been deposed by the forces of Francisco Madero. Madero, son of a wealthy Mexican landowner, schooled in revolutionary ideals while an art student in Paris, was a gifted agitator but a blind politician; he rose to power only to have his family and friends corrupt his new government and ideals. Eventually he was killed and the revolutionary forces in Mexico split, following two leaders—Pancho Villa, a bandit and guerrilla warrior, and Venustiano Carranza, a former follower of Madero—against the dictator, Victoriano Huerta.

President Wilson, being a liberal, refused to recognize Huerta, but was uncertain where to place the power that would go with United States' recognition. Steffens, approaching the entire situation from a Marxist leaning, concluded that the easiest method to determine the genuine leader of the people was to find whom the bankers supported and, eliminating their choice by default, study and possibly support the other man. Since Wall Street forces were united behind Villa, studying Carranza, Steffens decided, would teach him more about "the revolution." Villa, he rightfully assumed, had the support of Wall Street only because it felt he could be controlled; Villa's success would mark the people's—"the revolution's"—failure.

Many of Steffens's findings in Mexico were similar to his findings in the muckraking years. Villa, the bandit, was, for example, parallel to the political boss of a city—a man willing to do the dirty work capitalists needed done and yet would not do themselves. Indeed, Steffens's analysis of Mexico was, in form and substance, a logical extension of his muckraking of American cities and states. He used his conclusions from those years as axioms upon which to build analysis of the revolution, and he judged men by comparison to established standards. For example, in an article entitled "Making Friends With Mexico," published in *Collier's* in 1916, he wrote that "the Mexican people were voted under Diaz somewhat as our people used to be voted: by the machine and the lesser leaders of the system. And now, under Carranza, the Mexicans will probably have to go all through that slow process we have been going through, to learn how to vote themselves."[1] In a letter to his sister he echoed the same sentiment: "As I have told you before, it's the same old story that we have had in the cities and states of the U.S."[2]

Mexico, however, was clearly another country. Steffens objected to the extension of the United States' social standards over our Southern neighbor. Our expansionist arrogance —our "white man's burden"—he found particularly galling, since he was certain of our own moral shortcomings. Of the applicaton of our provincial ideals to Mexican life he wrote, "We, sure of the superior excellence of ours, we continually thrust ours upon them—our ideals, our ideas, our virtues, and also (as they see) our vices, and our methods, and our corruption; and all for their good. This is the height of our offending: our philanthropy."[3]

Steffens was, in fact, cynical about all foreign intentions in Mexico. Outside concern, he believed, was only an extension of foreign greed. He thought Mexico a dream land, "a Garden of Eden: a beautiful, great, warm country where nobody need work very hard."[4] The Puritan work ethic and its implications—especially for selfish, imperialistic motives—was not needed. It was rather the catalyst for revolution. One of the things Steffens was proudest of, as noted in his *Autobiography*, was his part in the revitalizing of an old Mexican law claiming that the purchase of land did not include the purchase of mineral rights under the surface, a law which was to plague many oil-hungry foreign ministers and investors.[5]

Steffens held a unique position in Mexico; he was a pro-Marxist, pro-Mexican American, whose opinion was respected by Carranza (if not the entire revolutionary force), and who was also respected by the powers in Washington. Carranza, in an attempt to evade forces that would corrupt and, simultaneously, find out the opinions of the Mexican people, loaded his entire government on a train that moved about Mexico, always a few steps ahead of foreign businessmen. Steffens was one of the few Americans on the train, and was most certainly the most trusted.[6] His discretion and Mexican sympathies allowed him to go where other reporters could not, since he was quite thoroughly rid of his imperialistic bias. Carranza eventually suggested that Steffens aid in the work of his constitutional committee. It is quite impossible to measure the degree of his help, though he denies it was very extensive. But, discounting any influence he may have had, it is a good sign of Carranza's trust that Steffens—a reporter from the United States—was allowed to attend the meetings of the revolutionary government.[7]

While encouraged by what he saw in Mexico, Steffens was discouraged by the course of events in the United States. Generally speaking, businessmen and the press were urging intervention. Wilson, in Steffens's opinion, was dangerously shielded from the true facts by capitalistic elements in Washington. Steffens, possibly in an attempt to raise a strong public opposition to capitalistic lobbying, made no attempt to hide his opinions about intervention. He praised the Carranza government and underscored the errors of the United States' foreign policy. In May 1916, in an article in *Everybody's,* he wrote first of intervention: "It's treason we are talking about: international treason, treason to Mexico in Mexico and treason to the United States in the United States," and secondly, in italics, of the Carranza government: "*Señor Carranza and his inner circle of advisors are as sincere, as honest, as determined, and—as perplexed a group of radical reformers as I ever saw (or heard of or read about) in power.*"[8]

Steffens was quite aware of the difficulties plaguing the emerging Mexican government. In May 1916 he wrote to his sister that the Carranza supporters "woefully lack[ed] competence, executive and organizing ability, and economic understanding." He also knew that his opinions were not going to be accepted objectively, as they once had been. "The editors," he wrote, "won't like some of my generalizations. For example: I am more than ever convinced that the social problems will not be solved by good men and intellectuals, but by intellectuals, practical men and many, many rascals; . . . And, therefore, we waste time demanding virtue from our reformers. . . ."[9] Steffens was clearly aware that his words no longer stung as they once had; the McNamara case still haunted him, and his new radical leanings were not hidden or checked at all.

Nonetheless, he played a role in averting a war with Mexico. Finding that President Wilson was wrongfully convinced that Carranza wanted war, he made a successful grandstand play and convinced the President that his advisers' opinions were too narrow. A commission was finally established to settle the Mexican dispute, based at least in part on plans formulated by Steffens. The group consisted of six men, three from Mexico and three from the United States, to settle Mexican-American disagreements. Steffens balked at being one of the members, but he played a liaison role, making sure that both sides were represented by men sympathetic to a just settlement for Mexico. According to Steffens's account of the affair, Wilson credited him with the prevention of a war with Mexico.[10]

Wilson was impressed with Steffens's efforts, thinking him among the best-informed men on the Mexican situation. This, no doubt, was significant later when Steffens was allowed to go into Russia with the quasi-official "Bullitt Mission," after the Russian Revolution broke. Steffens was also asked to write anonymously a chapter on the Mexican situation for inclusion in a campaign book on Wilson to be issued in the 1916 presidential fight. Though he finished the chapter, party officials became fearful of Steffens's radical stand and of the association of Steffens's ideas with the President's election. They squelched the chapter.[11]

While the dramatic impact of the Russian Revolution and its consequences would soon dwarf the importance of what happened in Mexico, Steffens's role in shaping United States' foreign policy and his power as an effective liberal-radical force in governmental affairs was certainly greater in 1916 than it would be for the rest of his life. It was, for a brief moment, almost as it had been ten years earlier. But involvement in the war in Europe was to reshape American priorities—especially in foreign affairs—and the idealistic working of individual radicals would soon be considerably lessened.

Steffens had gone to Mexico, he wrote his sister, to learn about the nature of "the revolution; not only the Mexican revolution, but the very same they had in France and long[ed] for in England and Germany and Russia."[12] While he never listed all his conclusions on revolution as determined from the Mexican affair, several generalizations emerge from his writing.

First, revolution in practice differed from revolution in theory. On his first trip to Mexico Steffens met a group of departing foreign revolutionaries who had toured Mexico and were going home "to report that the Mexican revolution was not a 'veritable' revolution; it was not going according to

Marx." Steffens soon saw that the idealized theories of revolutionaries, like those of the reformers in the United States,
had blinded them to the essence of the revolt; they could not
see the greatness because they were concerned with the
trivialities of theory.[13] Because of this observation, Steffens
managed in later situations to evade blanket theoretical statements that might illustrate dogmatic belief in any theory. He
was not a blind believer in communism for very long; his
mind and his experience were always quick to supply con-
tradictions to any hardening theory.

Second, and closely related, Steffens understood the distinct
separation of the theoreticians from the soldiers in a revolution. The men fighting were after their enemy—in the form
of people and places—rather than against "the System." This
is not to say that they were unfamiliar with the theories involved, although that may often have been the case—merely
that they did not fight concepts, they fought battles. As he
wrote in one article:

A revolution is a confusing, fierce, and revolting force. It isn't what
the theoretical revolutionists seem to expect. It's militarism. . . . The
soldier's instincts and his orders are to destroy. But he doesn't destroy what revolutionists would destroy. The soldier only destroys
everything he can lay his hands on. He destroys men, not ideas,
women and virtue, not prostitution and vice; buildings, not institutions; courthouses, not injustice; bridges, tracks, and cars, not railroad charters and corruption; growing crops and landlords, not the
landlord and the unfair land tenure.[14]

It should be added that even the men leading the revolution,
at least in Mexico, were basically fighters and dreamers rather
than tightly trained Marxist functionaries. In his *Autobiography*
Steffens added that "neither Madero nor Carranza was a
well-grounded radical; they were not clear economists, and
they did not see that to carry out the many drastic political
and the superficial few economic changes they proposed
would require great political wisdom and profound revolutionary reforms."[15] Obviously theory was secondary to military

ability; it seemed better to eliminate the bad with no definite plans for the future than live under a most certainly bad present. In fact, theory could come after the overthrow of the old order was over, as current experience has illustrated.

Third, revolution is often ended by a peace that does not achieve the theoretical goals that the dreamers envisioned. Its goals may have changed or been misdirected, or it may have started with a wrong premise. Even if a revolution ends with less than expected, however, it usually leads to another revolution, a step in a painful journey. When the peace in Mexico was signed, Steffens wrote to his sister that he knew it would not last, for it "didn't touch the basic cause of war. . . ."[16] In short, he assumed it rare for a revolution to be successful in attaining its original goals, or even maintaining them.

Fourth, Steffens was reaffirmed in his belief that social change followed a predictable pattern. His comparison of the causes and effects of unrest in Mexico to similar cause-effect relationships he had observed in the United States merely reinforced this opinion. Predictability, obviously, was in keeping with the Marxist application of historical evidence to the formulation of rules of social science. He felt it significant that "man could use history as an applied science." "The real trouble with us," he wrote, "is that we Americans are not taught the experimental. We say 'history repeats itself' as if it were a fatalistic law of nature."[17] History, in Marxist perspective, was a tool. If similar conditions led to similar reactions, historians could determine to which stage of development a society had progressed in relation to other societies and, assuming man has some influence over social conditions, determine the direction that society would follow by altering social conditions responsible for change. While there are faults to this logic, there are also strengths. For a man who wants to change the world it is almost an essential opinion. Steffens's years of dealing with the United States made economic determinism seem unavoidably obvious.

Fifth, and reinforcing the idea that revolutions evolved

from specific causes, Steffens felt that "the revolutionists cannot make a revolution. Only a government, only the established order, can make a revolution. . . ." Revolutionists could cause disorder, but they would succeed only where intrinsic conditions were sufficiently bad. Revolution was caused by the faults of the old order, not by the propaganda of radicals. "The Mexican revolution," he believed, "was already made long before an incident started it. A revolution is, in that respect, like a war."[18] Obviously there would always be people unhappy with the status quo; what was necessary, however, was a government removed enough from the people to force the citizens in the direction determined by organized revolutionists. If the people were happy no amount of mere talk would force them to change. Government sprang from conditions, and conditions had to be bad before new governments evolved.

Sixth, and quite obvious, Steffens learned the functional difficulties involved in executing a revolution—much as he had learned that there were subtle complications involved in reform that were never apparent to the untrained observer. The followers of Carranza, for example, were soon as guilty of corruption as the men they had deposed, because they were placed in positions where they were offered the same temptations. Once again, good men soon became bad men because they were human. Also, Carranza himself was not able in economic matters. He was a competent statesman, but that was only of secondary significance, considering the emphasis Marxism placed on economic determinism. Since Carranza never destroyed the capitalistic frame of reference, he never achieved what Steffens considered the aim of the revolution.

The Mexican Revolution was Steffens's first encounter with active, physical revolution, and thus was important. Upon its conclusion he was a full-fledged expert, knowledgeable in theory and practice as much as any political analyst could be. When he went into Russia, he could speak with greater assurance than the typically untraveled American journalist of the times. The similarities between the Mexican and the Russian Revolution are few, but Steffens had learned enough to make the larger conflict comprehensible.

The Russian Revolution

Steffens journeyed to Russia twice, in late March 1917 and in mid-February 1919. Each trip increased his faith in the soundness of socialism as the political direction of the future and in the sincerity of the Russian people's attempt at radical reform. So great was the influence of these trips that one must change the way in which he views Steffens's actions after 1917. The Russian Revolution altered his perception of the world more than any other single historic event.

Mexico had set the stage, but the impact of its revolution was minute in comparison. His experience in Mexico had, in a sense, seasoned his liberal inclinations, adjusting his palate to the strong flavor of revolution. But the Mexican Revolution, as Steffens observed it, had remained largely political, a matter of governments and individuals. Russia, on the other hand, served up a seven-course meal. The revolution there was a social, cultural, intellectual, and political experience. No longer was it merely governmental maneuvering that Steffens was observing, but a world remade. (Indeed, he soon dismissed the formal government of Russia as an ineffectual body relating little to the revolution.) The Russian people, like a great Russian bear, swept all institutions away with grand disregard for tradition, leaving even new, liberal government, in Steffens's words, "high and dry." Moderate reform would no longer suffice; the revolution baptized Steffens into the long-awaited new order. "The System," in Russia at least, had been defeated.

Steffens's first trip began just days before America declared her entry into the war in Europe. Going out of personal curiosity, tied to no journalistic or governmental duties, the fifty-one-year-old reporter felt free to wander at will through

Petrograd, observing first the government of such men as Milyukov and, after dismissing that, sessions of the Soviet, that large free-floating council of revolutionaries that, albeit unofficially, represented, Steffens thought, the will, hopes, power, and future of the Russian people.

The main lesson of his first trip was that Russia faced a dilemma springing directly from her extreme democracy. The so-called revolutionary government that had replaced the old nobility floundered hopelessly because it was a remnant of the old order—more liberal than anything before, but still mentally bound to capitalism. "Those fine, honest, highly educated gentlemen never understood that our liberalism is only an attempt to moderate the workings of a system which was then at war," Steffens recalled when writing his *Autobiography*. "Their culture, their propaganda, had never attempted to visualize what might be done if the system itself were wiped out and they had a clean slate on which to draw another system."[19]

And so, ignoring her leaders, the Russian mass vacillated precariously between arguing factions, and, with the rest of the world at war, accomplished nothing. Every judgment the would-be leaders made was immediately publicized and turned against them, if not by one faction then by another, creating a paradox: in the United States democracy had been so thwarted that it had ended, in Steffens's interpretation, in a dictatorship of business; in Russia, however, democracy was so literal that it led to chaos and indecision. Steffens preferred the latter, since it held at least the promise of the best as well as of the worst.

The Allies, however, disapproved. When they turned to Milyukov and later Krenski to lead Russia against the Germans, they were sorely disappointed. Why, they wondered, didn't these Russians follow their own leaders?

Since he held a unique position—being a known reporter, knowledgeable about and sympathetic toward the Soviet cause, and not affiliated with any position that required his presence in Russia—Steffens was asked by Charles Crane, the man he had gone to Russia with, and American Ambassador David

Francis, to make Russia's reasons for nonentry into the war clear to the Allies; thus, his first trip ended sooner than expected. The Wilson administration, painfully short on firsthand information, as it had been in the Mexican crisis as well, needed information only Steffens could supply.

Crossing Siberia, Japan, and the Pacific, Steffens reached Washington by mid-June, where he reported his beliefs to the President and, more fully, to presidential adviser Colonel Edward M. House. In one of his letters to House he spelled out his interpretation of the Soviet position toward the war:

The Russians can be made to fight, but only by an act of the Allies. In a highly exalted state of mind, the effect of the revolution, they think that if all the Allies would reduce their purposes (or raise them) to a demand only for permanent peace (no punishments; no compensations; no extension of territory; and a promise to let the question of the sovereignty of the lesser nations be answered by the lesser nations), then we could have peace. And if we couldn't, if Germany refused to hear on this basis, then,—then the Russians would fight.

It may be an illusion, but the Russians think they are asked now to fight, not to achieve idealistic ends, but to carry out certain secret treaties among certain of the Allies. Whatever it is, illusion or fact, this belief and the psychological condition of the Russian mind are facts which should and can be dealt with, if understood.[20]

But the Soviet would not continue to fight to preserve a world order it had rejected. It felt no duty to honor treaties, especially imperalistic ones, made by the government so recently overthrown. Part of the reason the Russian masses refused to follow the new government was that government's willingness to continue the war. The desire of the Western nations to make the people of Russia fight revealed only the ulterior motives of capitalism, or so it seemed to a people so recently freed from the almost feudal conditions of Czarist Russia. "It was," Steffens thought, "a comic and also a tragic show, that provincial government's efforts, at our behest, to force a people who, newborn to freedom, as they thought, interested in a revolution full of possibilities—land, liberty, justice, and permanent peace with all the world—to carry on a war that they were through with against their very good friends, the German workers and peasants."[21] No longer nation against nation, it was now class against class, until there be no more classes.

The Russian Revolution fulfilled the dreams of not only the Russian peasants, Steffens felt, but of all mankind. It presented an object lesson from which the rest of the world could learn how to govern. In a short story entitled "Midnight in Russia," published in *McClure's* soon after Steffens returned, the story is told of a young, second-generation Russian-American Jew who returned to Russia to fight for the revolution. In that fight he sees his dreams for democracy and he explains the revolution as a guidepost to a better tomorrow. The economic class structure of America contradicts the dreams his father, as an immigrant, had trusted. " 'Now I understand,' " the young revolutionary explains his concept of what was wrong in America, " 'that if you start a country off wrong underneath—economically wrong; not as a commonwealth for the common good, but each for himself and the mines and the lands for the firstcomer—then, of course, labor must organize to force the workers to unite for the good of all.' "[22] Democracy could not exist, as explained, in a country where wealth was not held by the people as a whole—in short, by the state. Since freedom depended on the financial ability of a person to do whatever he desired, uneven distribution of wealth ensured uneven distribution of freedom. The life of the fictional Russian-American Jew in the New York ghetto illustrated full well to Steffens the fallacy of the concept of equal opportunity and the essential flaw in the Horatio Alger rags-to-riches theory. America had appeared not as a dream but as a nightmare to the young revolutionary; and the Russian Revolution—which aimed at the elimination of private property and the establishment of a commonwealth—became the hope of the future, as America's Revolution had been the hope of the past.

Thus, when the government of Russia changed, and became representative of the common people (or, literally became the

common people, as Steffens viewed it), the goals of the government changed. People no longer fought for the same objectives; now the poor of all nations were seeking democracy
from the wealthy, who were defending (in the World War) the
system that had allowed them to become wealthy. And so,
when the Russian peasants heard that they were fighting to
honor secret treaties that would give them new property, they
refused to continue. That land belonged to the peasants of
other lands, and there was no justice in seizing it. The old
government, not the people, had wanted it. Governments,
especially capitalistic governments, were at the root of all
problems. As Steffens's young revolutionary put it, government was " 'the thing that killed my father in America, and
my grandfather, my grandmother in Russia; and in Germany
made this war. And you come over here, you Americans, you
Allies, and you advise us to hurry up and set up
—government; and a police; and labor unions; and an army.
And you wonder that we won't do it, that the Russians say
no?' "[23]

This mixture of communism and anarchism formed into the
lesson Steffens returned to the United States ready to teach.
He could not have chosen a worse time. Only a few months
into the war, seized by nationalism and the rightness of their
cause, the American public was not anxious to hear that their
own government had duped them into defending a false
democracy; nor did they readily believe that their education
had deceived them into a distorted sense of freedom. When
Steffens's peasant asked, " 'How can you be free if you think
you are free; how can you become a democracy if you think
you are one?' " he was facing himself squarely against popular
sentiment.[24] Was not this the "war to end all wars," "the war
to make the world safe for democracy"?

Thus, when Steffens toured the United States lecturing on
the Russian Revolution he lost even more of the public's favor.
He attributed part of his unpopularity to the effect of the war.
To Robert La Follette he wrote that the war fever was "a
sickness. . . . Individuals I talked with who had it, showed that

they had lost their moorings. The war has swept away their religion or their philosophy, rolled flat all the grooves on which all their thinking has been done. They are confused; in doubt about the righteousness of their cause. . . ."[25] On several occasions his reputation preceded him, causing his lecture to be canceled or his audience to be hostile. In another letter he noted, "I'm not arrested yet. . . . There have been sheriffs present, and Federal stenographers have taken down my lectures for some official reading."[26] While he assured everyone that his talks concerned Russia and not the war, the implications of his viewpoint were more than obvious. Quite clearly, he must have understood the reaction that Americans would have, considering that they were fighting a world war to preserve their own way of life. He would have been naïve indeed had he expected his message to be welcomed as a description of the way of the future.

The Bullitt Mission

Steffens's second trip to Russia began on February 22, 1919. In Paris to report on the Peace Conference, he suggested to Colonel House that a quasi-official mission could be sent discretely to the leaders of the new Russian government in an attempt to draw them into the settlement. The delegates at Versailles shared a general fear that if some effort was not made to co-opt the Russian impetus, the revolution that had started there would soon engulf all of Europe. The first suggestion on how to deal with the new government—a conference of the various nations on the island of Prinkipo—met with no success and, fearing an ineffective peace that ignored Russia and ensured a relapse to imperialism, Steffens suggested that a secret mission to sound out Bolshevik feeling and to outline to the Bolsheviks the Peace Conference's goals would do no harm and could be officially denied if it accomplished no good.

Although House originally thought it best that Steffens not be among the group selected to go, the liberal journalist even-

tually was included, probably because it would be easy to re-
pudiate someone with Steffens's reputation if repudiation became necessary. The man selected to lead the group was William C. Bullitt, a young blue-blood then working for the State
Department, who was openly sympathetic to liberal causes and
particularly interested in the Russian Revolution. He and Steffens would become firm friends. Two other men, an ex-social
worker and military man, Captain W. Petit of United States
Military Intelligence, and a naval secretary named Lynch,
completed the group. Lynch left the group before it entered
Russia, and Petit remained in Petrograd, the first stop in the
Russian tour, leaving Bullitt and Steffens to proceed to
Moscow—and Lenin.

Since his return from his first Russian trip, and despite all
his enthusiasm for what he had seen, Steffens had begun to
question his original opinions concerning the implications of
mass rule. Change had continued in Russia, most noticeably
the swift rise of the Bolsheviki, and when he returned for a
second look he changed many of his conclusions.

The replacing of the Krenski, or "white Russian," government by the Bolshevik, or "red Russian," government dis-
turbed the delegates at the Peace Conference. The reds were
more radical, and their takeover had been ruthless; also,
which government should be recognized as officially representing the Russian people? While the "whites" minded the official organs of government, the "reds," under Lenin, had become the *de facto* rulers.

Although Steffens was enamored by the democracy of the
masses on his first trip, he was convinced on his second trip
that dictatorship had become essential; the fumbling crowd
had found no direction, moving aimlessly and effectively
squelching any possibility for success. What was needed, if
only temporarily, was a dictator who could give the Soviet
purpose and direction. During Steffens's absence Lenin had
filled that role, and when Steffens observed the effect of the
man he was convinced of the rightness of his method. To his
friend Marie Howe, and to others, he admitted, "It is the most

absolute dictatorship I have ever seen," but he added immediately that "the leaders of it know that, they don't like it either, and they mean to change it later when they have used their power to force the economic revolution which is their first objective."[27]

Staying in Russia only about two weeks, Steffens moved quickly, seeing as many government leaders as possible. Having no specific duties, as the other members of the mission did, he was able to review the revolutionary movement as a whole. He wrote a friend, "We saw everybody we wished to see, saw everything we asked to see, heard all their story. . . . I had talks with Lenin, Trotzky [*sic*] and all the other men and women you have heard the names of, and many others besides."[28] He reported the integrity of the cause: "Lenin eats, like everybody esle, only one meal a day—soup, fish, bread, and tea. . . . The people, the peasants, send him more, but he puts it in the common mess. So the heads of this government do not have to imagine the privations of the people; they feel them."[29]

He was also convinced that the violent stage of the revolution was over. More than anything else, it had been that—"the terror"—that had made the Russian Revolution terrible to the Peace Commission. The commissioners, like most people in Europe at that time, felt quite certain that a much larger revolution was in the offing, and they were terrified. Steffens was also convinced that the regrettable terror had been necessary for the ultimate achievement of the revolution's goals —goals he was himself beginning to believe. He was thinking in Marxist terminology: "not political democracy, as with us; economic democracy is the idea; democracy in the shop, factory, business," he wrote. "Bolshevism is a literal interpretation, the application of this theory, policy, or program. And so, in the destructive period of the Russian Revolution, the Bolshevik leaders led the people to destroy the old system, root and branch, fruit and blossom, too. And apparently this was done. . . . It is this that startled the world, not the atrocities of the Revolution, but the Revolution itself."[30]

It had been the general chaos of "the terror" that had allowed the Soviets to accomplish substantial change. "While the mob broke windows, smashed wine cellars, and pillaged buildings to express their rage," wrote Steffens, "their leaders directed their efforts to the annihilation of the system itself. They pulled down the Czar and his officers; they abolished the courts, which had been used to oppress them; they closed shops, stopped business generally, and especially all competitive and speculative business; and they took over all the great industries, monopolies, concessions, and natural resources."[31] The chaos was, in effect, merely surface; under it the Communists proceeded with the orderly, extensive, and effective dismantling of capitalism.

Steffens rightly predicted that the new order would endure rather than end in another revolution. He understood the desire for reform, having himself been a reformer, and could sense the sincerity of Russian radicalism. The new government rested soundly upon layer after layer of local Soviets. Lenin was in firm control; "a majority of all the soviets in all Russia would have to be changed in personnel or opinion, recalled, or brought somehow to recognize and represent the altered will of the people," declared Steffens, in order to remove the new dictator.[32]

Two weaknesses in the new system escaped Steffens's notice and, in a sense, reveal something of the blind faith and optimism he held toward the revolution. First, although Lenin was far removed from the people, Steffens never suggested that his power could stem from or end as a result of political intrigue among politicos rather than from sincere public sentiment. Steffens seemed to believe that only massive public action could cause change; he was blind to the security that the new bureaucracy offered to ambitious men. Second, he forgot that power corrupts. The revolutionaries, as he saw them, were all idealists. "It is," he said, "as if we should elect in the United States a brand-new set of men to all offices, from the lowest county to the highest federal position, and as if the election should occur in a great crisis, when all men are full of hope and faith."[33] He must have concluded that the abolition of capitalism had included the abolition of ambition for power. As later events in Russia would show, such was not the case.

It is ironic that a political observer of Steffens's ability and experience failed to see the particular weaknesses that had been so responsible for the failure of reform in the United States. Had not he seen time and again that the activity of a state or city government did not respond to the wishes of the people because of a bureaucracy that had been built to shelter the men in power? And even more obvious, had not man after man in the United States entered politics with honorable intentions only to gradually, often unknowingly, but steadily become a part of the system he had intended to reform? Is not this very problem a major factor in the decline of the Progressive movement; and wasn't Steffens, more acutely than most, sensitive to the shortcomings—in his eyes the failure —of reform?

If he did see these shortcomings, he suppressed his knowledge of them, probably because of something else he saw: the Communists had a long-term operating plan that overrode daily concerns. Lenin himself explained it to Steffens. Taking a pencil and paper, "he drew a straight line: 'That's our course, but' —he struck off a crooked line to a point—'that's where we are. That's where we have had to go, but we'll get back here on our course some day.' He paralleled the straight line."[34] That was the vision that stuck in Steffens's mind, and with it was a firm opinion of Lenin as the scholar, the architect, and the hero of the new Russia. Steffens had attempted to coordinate a long-term reform in Boston, and he recognized a good administrator. In Lenin the Soviets had found a man who knew when he began what he was after, a rare quality by itself. But combined with that quality, Lenin had persuasion and brilliance, and was capable of operating a society like an engineer with a blueprint. Not merely content with hopes, he had seen that success depended on foresight founded on bedrock ability.

A liberal who had successfully led his country to a new order, politically, economically, and culturally, Lenin had traits that made him seem almost saintly to Steffens. Most noticeably, Lenin had attained a point at which he stopped questioning his ideas and began acting upon them. But other men had and would impress Steffens in a like way. It was the combination of this element with others that made Lenin seem so special. First, Lenin was a liberal. He was acting from concern for the people he represented rather than from a desire to help business or capitalism; such a competent dictator as Mussolini, whom Steffens also respected for ability, could not make the same claim. A dynamic and determined man, Lenin was sincere in his conviction that the people would be better off as a result of his efforts. Second, Lenin had the ability to adapt his methods without compromising his goals. While he might veer from his straight line, he would never adjust the original goal.

Belief in the Russian government's desire to remain true to its original goals remained with Steffens. In the 1930's he commented that "the only fault from a Western point of view in Russian concessions to outside capitalists who come into Russia and develop business is that they are not in perpetuity. The Soviet terms require [that] . . . Russia can take back the property by the payment of a handsome price, previously arranged."[35]

Soon Bullitt reached a suitable understanding with Soviet officials, settling most of the points that had, according to Lloyd George and Colonel House, concerned the peace delegates. Historian N. Gordon Levin has conveniently listed the proposed agreement as follows: "a stationary armistice in the civil war, a withdrawal of foreign troops from Russia, an establishment of trade relations between the Soviets and the Allies, and a pledge of political moderation in their foreign and domestic policies by the Soviet authorities in European Russia."[36] Satisfied that they had everything they had intended to get, Bullitt and his associates returned to Paris, confident that they had the solution to the Soviet problem.

But their success with the Soviets was not matched by success at home. Political pressures, in both England and the United States, worked quickly to deny the liberal Bullitt group their success.

In England, Lloyd George was confronted with the possibility of being labeled a radical by the conservative press of Lord Northcliffe and opposition in Parliament under Winston Churchill. Fearful of the consequences of being associated with two obvious Soviet sympathizers—Bullitt and Steffens—he denied to Parliament any connection with the Bullitt Mission.

Dealing with Wilson proved even more complex. American arrangements had all been made by Colonel House, who proceeded under the assumption that Wilson, in seeking the original Prinkipo conference, agreed that *de facto* recognition should be given the Bolsheviki. Fearing the power of a unified Russia, House believed that recognizing the existence of the Bolshevik government in the context of the Bullitt agreement would contain the Communists (by terms of the agreement) and divide Russia into smaller, less awesome threats. With this as a working thesis, he and Philip Kerr, secretary to Lloyd George, had composed the terms Bullitt had secured. (These terms, however, were basically the same as those the Bolsheviki had unsuccessfully proffered the Peace Commission two months earlier.)

But House had misread Wilson's desires. Convinced that Russia could and should be reunited under the liberals (or "whites") rather than the radicals (or "reds"), Wilson decided against giving recognition to the *de facto* government. Rather, he threw his support behind a food relief plan proposed by Herbert Hoover that would illustrate the United States' concern for the welfare of the Russian people without aiding the Bolsheviki with recognition. Part of Wilson's reluctance to recognize the "reds" probably came from pressure in the United States similar to the pressure that had affected Lloyd George; there was a growing "red scare" in America that Wilson was very much aware of; and he was advised by both Secretary of State Robert Lansing and Undersecretary Frank L. Polk that he could ill afford close association with Bolshevism. Upon reading the Bullitt plan, Polk wired from Washington, "I do not think I would be prepared to act on any report framed by Bullitt and Steffens after a three days' stay in Russia."[37]

With all their hopes dashed, Bullitt and Steffens gave up. Bullitt left for the Riviera; Steffens, who thought Wilson was bungling the whole affair by not admitting failure, turned to private concerns, rejecting the foolishness of a system that, he believed, had not learned the lesson World War I had taught.

But he had gained from the entire experience a new love—Communist Russia. As he grew older, his opinion of the strengths and weaknesses there would alter, and his hopes for the United States would markedly improve; but he saw the Soviets as the leaders of a Progressive world. The United States, most specifically after World War I, was firmly entrenched in the old "System," founded on an outdated economic theory. His own famous statement best sums up his feelings: "I have seen the future, and it works."

Prophet of Communism

After watching two revolutions and trying to understand their significance, Steffens did eventually reach some tentative conclusions, which are best summarized in a short book he wrote between 1923 and 1925 called *Moses in Red.* It is an analogy comparing modern revolution—the Russian Revolution in particular—with the story of Moses and the Exodus of the Jews from Egypt, as told in the Old Testament.

Intrinsic to his analysis, in fact the central premise of his entire thesis, is the belief that human progress is subject to a logical, scientifically observable order. He felt that "revolutions, like wars, are social-economic explosions due to human (political) interference with natural (and, therefore, divine) laws and forces which made for gradual growth or constant change called evolution."[38] The world progressed by natural laws, and, since man can determine the workings of those laws through observation and history, he can use them for his benefit.

In holding this belief Steffens was merely reflecting a liberal strain prevalent in the American historiography of his times. Such works as Charles Beard's *An Economic Interpretation of the Constitution,* published in 1913, or the collection of essays by James Harvey Robinson entitled *The New History,* published in 1912, start with the same assumption. The effect of an imported method of seminar history teaching was starting to be felt; no longer could history be considered mere chance or divine guidance. While once the domain of American aristocrats, history was evolving into a science. The question of whether history was a science or an art, which is still an issue, was beginning to be asked. Adherents of the newer view that history was a science—generally labeled "economic determinists"—believed that wars, revolutions, indeed all human events, were predictable if the conditions involved were scientifically analyzed. Consequently, history was no longer events of world-shaking proportion; rather, it was the study of those day-to-day conditions that led to great events. This, in part, is why Steffens felt he had to prepare to study revolutions—he had to understand them in the larger, socio-economic context. "We have to make a science of sociology," he thought, "and we cannot do that so long as we look upon some social events with horror." Thus, his job as social critic and historian was to compare all aspects of as many revolutions as he could observe, either via history or in person, and in the end make some rules about revolutions and progress. The revolutions had not been unique or unexplainable; they had been logical consequences.

Obviously Steffens, or any other historian holding these views, was unpopular with the increasingly conservative middle class of the 1920's. The ultimate goal of their attempts at understanding would be, of course, the shaping of a better future from the lessons history taught. The general public was undergoing a futile attempt to forget or ignore the implications of World War I, and adherence to any type of history so strongly dependent on the groundwork laid by Marx and so essential to his theories was bound to be unpopular. *Moses in Red* simply came too late to be well received (although it could be that it came too early). Its conclusions and implications cut too close to the public, which already felt threatened by the "Communist conspiracy." Besides, capitalism was entering its grandest decade, and critics would have a hard time convincing anyone of its weaknesses until October 10, 1929.

Nonetheless, there is strong American precedence for such an interpretation. Analysis of the laws of nature in order to understand the ways of the world was, after all, a central premise of the age of reason and of many of those men responsible for the American Revolution. Just as the work of Galileo and Newton had given rise to the liberal views of the seventeenth and eighteenth century as to the nature of the universe, so the work of Darwin and Freud gave rise to new liberal views of man's role in the universe in the twentieth century. Steffen's statement in *Moses in Red* that "according to science, which is the only living religion in the world today, all nature is a book of revelations, every laboratory experiment is a worship, and every natural phenomenon . . . is a sign of the hand, the voice, and the knowledge of God, and as such is to be respected," bears an uncanny similarity to much of the writing done by the fathers of the American Revolution. Revolution, after all, is a fairly American institution. Steffens was merely trying to determine those "laws of Nature and of Nature's God" that are referred to in the first paragraph of the Declaration of Independence. That his answer was more radical than others cannot be doubted, but neither can his intent to help mankind by his efforts. His logic is merely a twentieth century extension and application of Pope's dictum that

> All nature is but art, unknown to thee;
> All chance, direction, which thou canst not see
> All discord, harmony not understood;
> All partial evil, universal good;
> And spite of pride, in erring reason's spite
> One truth is clear, Whatever is, is right.

This is not to imply that Steffens condoned the excesses of the "red terror," or that other logical men could not disagree with him, but merely to contend that any phenomenon, such as the "red terror," was a logical product of the result of understandable rules. The "red terror," to continue the same example, was the final natural explosion caused because people tried to defy the natural evolution of the world's economic development. Steffens felt that capitalism had become outdated. If men understood the laws of nature and changed as the world did, rather than attempting to maintain outmoded forms of economy, the "terror"—in fact, the revolution itself—would never have come about. "The laws of nature hold through thick and thin," he declared, and if man fights them, revolution is inevitable. "There is some natural (divine) law discoverable," Steffens felt, "a set of causes which, once known to us, might enable wise leaders to manage a revolution without a Red Terror."[39]

In fact, nature struggled to avoid revolution. Steffens dismissed revolutionaries as not responsible for revolutions; they, like revolutions, were but responses to an imbalance in the world's natural evolution. The problem, as it had been in the muckraking days, was that the people in power attempted to create unnatural systems that would enable them to maintain their prominence after they no longer deserved it.

Inherited wealth, monopoly, and the excesses of capitalism all went headlong against the natural evolution of the true leaders of society and against true freedom. "Revolutionists do not make a revolution, . . ." Steffens decided. "History shows in its regular repetitions that the reactionary forces make what the revolutionists only prepare for. [Unnatural leaders and governments] drove the people to revolt."[40] The people endure far more than they deserve before they revolt, but they will eventually revolt if the natural progress of society is not allowed to go its way; again, such an opinion bears close resemblance to the Declaration of Independence.

Another point Steffens stressed in *Moses in Red,* and other places, was his belief that the older liberals who had worked for the revolution would themselves—and this meant Steffens himself—never reach the new world they fought for. While they realized the advantages of and the need for the new, the so-called old-guard liberals were too imbued with the ways of their own system; their instincts, their very gut reactions, were as conditioned as Pavlov's dogs to give them responses which, unfortunately, would be counter to the order they sought. When Emma Goldman, another American who had rushed to the support of the Communists in Russia, announced that she was disenchanted with life in Russia, Steffens wrote to a friend expressing his mixed emotions on his place in the new order: "Emma Goldman doesn't like Bolshevism in action, and wants to get back to free America. She is right. I had that feeling about Moscow and I came back to Paris, which I like. But I can see that it isn't important whether Emma and I get liberty. The important thing is that Bolshevik Russia shall go through its tyranny patiently and arrive at liberty for the whole Russian people and perhaps for the world. . . ."[41]

A new type of man was needed. Lenin provided the model; he had stopped intellectualizing and worrying about theory and, grabbing opportunity by its horns, had acted. He was, in consequence, a dictator. Steffens had observed in his muckraking years that really effective control of city government had come from individual "bosses" who did not have to bother with democratic niceties, and the memory of that truth must have figured in his determination of "a tentative statement of some such general law [of revolutions] as this: In revolutions, in wars, and in all such disorganizing, fear spreading crises in human affairs, nations tend to return to the first, the simplest and perhaps the best form of government: a dictatorship."[42] Such was one of the conclusions that could be reached by scientifically observing nature, and it must have come as quite a bitter pill for some of Steffens's friends to swallow. It is a long way from the brand of liberalism he had written in the Progressive era. But he made another conclusion which he called "a natural law of freedom" that, in a small way, explains why a dictatorship might be, at least temporarily, good: "Liberty is a state of freedom which, related in some way to the state of the public mind, increases in some ratio with the general sense of security and decreases in some similar ratio with the general sense of danger—regardless of man-made laws and soul-felt idealism."⁴³ Obviously liberty—still a cardinal virtue among liberals—could not exist in a revolutionary context, and its return would be facilitated by a dictatorship that could bring order and a sense of security out of a revolution-torn land.

There seems to be, however, something questionable in such a freedom. It is based on a view of the public that Steffens himself would hasten to deny. One cannot help feeling that such a "natural law of freedom" is derived from a belief that ignorance is bliss. The reader is forced to react negatively; it is far more typically American to agree with Franklin that those who would give up their freedom for temporary security deserve neither. Indeed, an unconscious air of superiority is implied by Steffens's attitude. When, for example, he writes that his "theory is that the righteous can be saved, that they do not have to be killed. It is only a matter of propaganda," his statements ring a tone of "big brother" too loudly for the American ear.⁴⁴ Is he not saying that there is an enlightened group that knows what is good for the "mob" that should be allowed to control propaganda and thus people? And is not implying such also implying that the majority needs to be controlled rather than in control? True, Steffens was not living in an age that had observed the power of Hitler, but the lessons of history must be objectively learned and not selectively chosen to suit one's hopes. Steffens's goal was freedom, and thus he deserves praise; but his method was no more foolproof than any others that have been offered (nor, it should be added, was it much worse than any others).

All things considered, *Moses in Red* is a blemish on Steffens's record, both as literature and as political theory. It is a cruel twist of irony that the same year Steffens tried to prove that Moses was the first Bolshevik, another author tried to prove that Christ was the first capitalist—each attempt failed philosophically. In 1925 Bruce Barton, an advertising agency

executive, published a book entitled *The Man Nobody Knows*
that bears some striking parallels to *Moses in Red*. Since
Barton's work reinforced the prevalent feelings of the times, it
was an unqualified commercial success. Like *Moses in Red*, it
attempted to interpret the work of God to prove divine
sanction for a particular economic system. For example,
Steffens compares Moses's wandering in the wilderness to the
jailing of the radicals from prerevolutionary Russia:

> The revolutionary leaders of Red Russia that have vital ideas are
> all ex-convicts. They thought themselves clear and sure in the solitary
> confinement of prisons. . . . The prophets of the Biblical revolts, all
> inspired of God, were led or sent away from among men to go off by
> themselves in order that they might communicate with Him Who
> seems, He alone, to have use for thinkers of thoughts that agitate.[45]

Such logic is, at best, well intended, and such comparisons,
while occasionally useful or enlightening, quickly reach an absurd point when forced to fit a preconception of right and
wrong.

The most telling thing about the two books is, as Professor
McLuhan would say, in the medium rather than in the message. Both propagandists—one for capitalism and the other
for communism—chose to convince the public of their points
of view via distorted versions of stories from the Bible. Steffens
was still a master of selecting a medium—as the success of
Barton's book indicated (a "best seller")—but he was out of
joint with the philosophy of his times. But, more interesting,
consider what assumptions can be made about the reading
public of the 1920's if such an approach was popular. Was it a
people trying to force their religion to fit their economic system so as to justify their methods, or was it a people trying
desperately to find a moral order in a world that seemed
more and more to have none? No doubt it was some subtle
combination of both; but, whatever the answer, the same questions apply to Steffens (and Barton, for that matter).

Steffens himself was not comfortable with communism, at
least in its nontheoretical, revolutionary form. He was sym-

pathetic toward Communist goals, and intellectually willing to accept their implications, but he was unable to abandon his past entirely. The twenties were hard years for Americans and their moral codes. The "golden calf" was on a higher altar in the boom years after the war than it had ever been. "The System" Steffens had analyzed and grown to detest was, in a very real way, in its golden age, giving its brightest explosion before the dark. It was paying unrealistically high dividends, and would continue to appear divine, as an economic system, until the bust in 1929.

CHAPTER 7

Artist

Altering the Pattern of Life

I N the years that elapsed between the end of the muckraking era and the beginning of the twenties, Steffens altered greatly his life-style. Beginning most noticeably after his wife's death, his acquaintances were more radical and intellectual than they had been, as his move to Greenwich Village would indicate.

His own intellectual attention shifted in those years from the popularization of political reform to an inquiry into the nature of revolutionary change. The men he had known during the muckraking years had been, at base, pillars of business and action who had entered politics for a mixture of practical and patriotic reasons. By the early teens, however, he mixed most often with men and ideas from outside the pale of popular reform; his circle of friends included more artists and authors, fewer businessmen and politicians.

Despite philosophic changes, however, he remained actively interested in politics through the teens, shifting his attention from the specifics of national politics to a broad overview of the international scene, reporting on revolutions and the peace efforts after the war. But by the beginning of the twenties, his perspective had once again changed noticeably. In his writing, both public and private, the political, cultural, and social events he studied were treated most often merely as examples—object lessons—to be used to illustrate generalizations and theories. Obviously, his life did not fit conveniently to any fixed pattern as an author might wish it to. But Steffens himself realized he had changed when he referred to one of his personal problems at that time. "Like so much else in life," he wrote to his sister, "like the lessons of my life and philosophy, this cannot be cloven into clean-cut parts, the good and the evil."[1] Comparison of any of his writings from 1916 with his writings of, say, 1923, illustrates the difference clearly.

Even *Moses in Red*, a distinctly political work, illustrates the nature of the shift. While he might earlier have noted an occasional similarity between a current event and some earlier event, he would never have devoted his entire story to examining the repetition of causes and events. Obviously he was coming to see the full implications of the system of government and society that he had himself helped to define. When one considers his belief in the scientific application of observed phenomena to prove theories concerning the nature of society—scientific history, for short—it is only logical that his interest in details declined as his concern with the nature of the whole increased. Having reported enough specific examples, he set out in the twenties to see what those examples all meant about life itself.

Thus, his role and position as a public figure also changed. In a piece entitled "Atlas: A Fable," written in 1923, Steffens recalled how he, as a child, had asked a teacher what Atlas stood upon as he held up the world. He received no good answer. But Atlas still puzzled him: his load was so heavy and his reward so mysterious. Steffens soon learned, he recounted, that the burdens of the world were on him also, and he grew to hate their weight. Until, he wrote, "One day, when my vanity was low, my horse sense high, and something else was a-borning, I declared (to myself) that I was through. It was too much. It wasn't fair. Let others bear their share. I would stand from under and let the darned thing go to the deuce."[2] And, starting in the early twenties, that is precisely what he did.

This is not to imply that he was no longer interested, that he deserted his opinions, or that he no longer kept his liberal guard high; it does mean, however, that he became much less a crusader and public figure and much more a private citizen. The effect is most apparent in his writings. His personal correspondence multiplied many times in volume, while his public writing became less concerned with news of the day and dealt, generally, with political, social, and cultural concepts in the abstract.

No longer a reporter of the news of the day, he became a philosopher instead of a journalist. His philosophy, it must be emphasized, was highly political (and heavily influenced by his journalistic training); he was never as successful in dealing with the abstract as he had been in dealing with the concrete. So he still found himself drawing from experience, now pointing out weaknesses in human nature rather than weaknesses in the political system.

Steffens's world travels contributed greatly to this shift in interests. His global experiences, especially in centers of radical and revolutionary change, forced upon him the habit of viewing the world order in terms of remodeling society. Now he began to concern himself with man in society.

"Peter"

There were also personal reasons for Steffens's altered lifestyle. He had tasted the rewards of success for years and no longer felt the need to prove himself to the world. At the beginning of his career he had fitted his life to the pattern society molded for him, spending weeks, often months, on the road away from his wife. But, by the time she died, he discovered that he had lost his desire to be what society expected him to be, and so he dismissed traditional modes of achieving success. Disgusted with what he saw "the System" doing to the state of world affairs, he had slowly but surely lost respect for tradition-bound ethics. He became an anarchist in social behavior, doing what experience taught him and dismissing "respectable" and "traditional" behavior as "bunk." (It should be added, however, that Steffens had a strong sense of proper conduct and public morality; his rejection of society's moral and behavioral code was not a total rejection of all codes; rather, it was a rejection of selective and questionable elements of that code.)

As mentioned earlier, he renewed an affair with a California woman (whom he had known from his California college days) after his wife's death. Because of numerous complications concerning her marriage, the difficulties of divorce, and his disdain for the Victorian morality of the times, he never married her. She offered him companionship and understanding, as is evident in his letters to her as well as in statements about her by contemporaries. Were this an intimate or personal biography, her role in his life would be significant. When he finally left her, he kept with him a sense of guilt derived from his shoddy treatment of her. He had broken his engagement to her when he had married the first time, and when history repeated itself he felt strongly the tragedy involved. When he wrote his *Autobiography* Steffens kept a promise by not mentioning her, but to his sister Laura he complained, "I promised, but it's too bad. What I really am is shown by that story better than any other. The whole [of the *Autobiography*] will be hurt by the omission." To his other sister he added, "If I tell only the professional tale of my life I shall be more a hero than, for example, [she] knows me to be or my sisters."[3] One can feel Steffens's sense of guilt best, perhaps, in another letter he wrote, claiming that "the tragedy of it is that I, the only villain, I got the best of it: it is the innocent that suffer."[4]

It appears that the California woman was holding onto a rather popular man in the early teens. Mable Dodge recalled that "in those days 'Steff—the little man—liked large equine women. One well-known woman had been a love of his. He had appeared on her horizon somewhere out west, and captivated her completely. But he seemed to like to dazzle their minds and then dance off . . . Steff's friends had to protect him from the determined women who went after him when he was through, claiming him, insisting upon his love, declaring they could not do their work unless he returned to them."[5]

But he eventually met a girl he could not forget. The cause of his leaving his California woman was a young graduate student at the London School of Economics, Ella Winter, whom he met in Paris in April 1919, soon after returning from the Bullitt Mission. She was working as a secretary to Harvard law professor and later Supreme Court Justice Felix Frankfurter, then chairman of the War Labor Policies Board, who was in Europe during the latter part of, and immediately following, the war. A close friend to Steffens, Frankfurter inadvertently brought the two together, beginning a slow burning affair that suffered both from Steffens's ties to another woman and Miss Winter's qualms about falling in love with the older and unconventional Steffens. After all, when they met he had just turned fifty-three and she was a very innocent twenty-one. Nevertheless, their affection was immediate and lasting. Soon after meeting her he wrote to his sister: "She's a brilliant girl from Australia, and I guess I'm her first girl-love and,—she's my first secretary."[6]

There is more to that statement than immediately meets the eye. While Steffen's first wife—a devoted and able woman——had worked hard to promote her husband's career, she was never a part of that career. Ella Winter, however, was a student of economics, highly educated, and an instinctive liberal; her inquisitive, studentlike interest, a perceptive political mind, along with natural ability as a journalist in her own right, complimented her expanding relationship and made her a part of Steffens's public and private life as his first wife had never been. She authored two books on life in Soviet Russia, and was an excellent translator. Her autobiography, *And Not to Yield,* is a sensitive and engaging volume.

Steffens felt no great urge to marry Miss Winter, whom he nicknamed "Peter," since he was accustomed to living as he felt rather than bending to custom. His affair with the California woman declined while his affair with Miss Winter grew, and only events that went beyond him served to force the issue. In 1923, after being barred from the British Empire for a few years, probably because he could expose Lloyd George's complicity in the very unpopular Bullitt Mission, Steffens returned to London where he actively revived his affair with Peter. After three months he convinced Peter to return to Paris with him. When, in early 1924, a doctor informed Steffens that she had lost her interest in him and her food because she was pregnant, the entire picture changed. Steffens, at age fifty-eight, was to be a father. His reaction was understandably mixed. Confused, he told her, " 'I'm an anarchist, I don't want the law to dictate to me,' " dismissing marriage as unnecessary. His second plan was to compromise with propriety, getting married and then divorced secretly. Eventually, with prodding from friends, he was convinced that the inconvenience was not worth the trouble, especially if they returned to the puritanical United States.[7] But, with the baby swiftly coming, Steffens rushed to put affairs right; when Peter was six months pregnant, they were married in Paris. Not until after his marriage, only months before his son was born, did Steffens effectively conclude his liaison with the woman from California.

Amid the Expatriots

From 1919, when he first met Peter, until he moved permanently back to the United States in March 1927, Steffens immersed himself in the intellectual and cultural world of postwar Europe and America—favoring Europe. His training in German universities plus his experience in the milieu of Mabel Dodge perfectly suited the intellectual ferment of the times. An established radical and avowed freethinker, he found that the company of such literary figures as John Dos Passos, Ernest Hemingway, James Joyce, Ezra Pound, Ford Maddox Ford, Gertrude Stein, e. e. cummings, H. G. Wells, and Sinclair Lewis complimented his temperament perfectly. An older and more recognized man of letters than most of the other American expatriots, his life of growing disillusionment with "the System" in America matched their disdain for post-war America.

With his close friend Jo Davidson he traveled across Europe, observing changes that were taking place, fitting them all carefully into his new, Socialist-Communist scheme of order. Steffens took Peter, both before and after their marriage, into his careful tutelage, a happy teacher with a willing student. He was young at heart again, starting a new life, but this time without the old inhibitions. Europe was just the place for learning what life really meant.

Living off the runaway profits of the American stock market, he deserted journalism, except for a short piece for an occasional liberal magazine with limited circulation. He was content to watch life, only rarely stopping to report some brief account, usually extolling the virtues of the Soveit Union or of Communist insights into the order of world politics. For a brief time in 1922, he substituted for the Hearst newspaper correspondent in Genoa, but generally he restricted his writing to philosophical letters to friends.

He took great interest in the young artists he met in Europe. He was among the first of the Americans to recognize the ability of Ernest Hemingway. Impressed both by the man and his prose, after Hemingway himself pointed out his ability, Steffens was, in the words of Hemingway's biographer Carlos Baker, "more than ever convinced that Hemingway had the surest future of any youngster on the European literary scene." So impressed was Steffens that he sent "My Old Man," one of Hemingway's early short stories, to Ray Long of *Cosmopolitan,* with a letter recommending the aspiring young author.[8]

After his marriage in 1924, Steffens moved with his young bride from Paris to San Remo, Italy (and later to Alassio), to a large, old, roomy country house, set in the hills overlooking a peaceful village. Because of his personal happiness, he found Italy's climate and people pleasant. Suprisingly, he was at first impressed by Benito Mussolini. Like the "bosses" from the big cities back home, or like Lenin in the Soviet Union, Mussolini had taken control of the situation as it existed, chaotic and aimless, and had molded it into a directed policy. Although he never moved to the right in sympathy, Steffens admired Mussolini's ability.

Disillusioned with democracy as he had seen it in America and blinded by admiration of Lenin's ability in achieving the goals of communism by avoiding democratic method, Steffens was questioning the degree to which democracy was either what people actually wanted or what they needed. By watching the Russians, Mussolini had observed that changing one's views to suit the needs of the times was a sure road to power, because, Steffens wrote, "no mere intellectual, he could change his mind, deep down, to the depths where it would change his acts, his every impulse." With no definite concept of how things should be—no intellectual ideal—Mussolini had the ability most intellectuals lacked and, Steffens felt, needed dearly: "Il Duce" could tailor his actions to reality instead of idealism and thus achieve realistic results.[9]

Comparing Lenin and Mussolini, he wrote that they had what the rest of the world's leaders needed: "The method is what we lack and need, a way to do what I had seen reformers at home (and in history) begin in vain to do. Where were we to learn how to succeed? Lenin had learned from history; Mussolini had learned from the news, confirmed by history, a way to do—whatever it was that they were doing, he and Lenin."[10] All Steffens's attempts at changing society had failed, and thus he respected the ability (if not always the motives) of anyone who succeeded in the attempt. His growing respect for the ability of the personally strong leaders, however, depended upon his growing disbelief in the democratic impulses of the people. In another place, a few years later, he wrote:

Mussolini met the observation that his people were indifferent to or against his war on Ethiopia by calling out 100,000 Romans to roar for the war. That should have shown us, but it didn't. Hitler could make his Germans cry for or against war any day. We saw President

Wilson turn practically all Americans from anti- to pro-war in a few weeks. People are potential pianos for a skilled performer till they go red, then they are no use to anybody. Hence our love of law and order.[11]

Certainly this doesn't say much for Steffens's opinion of the masses.

However, Steffens's admiration for Mussolini should not be confused with a liking for what the man did. Even the admiring Steffens chafed under his rule, and his experiences with Communist philosophy did not prepare him to accept Fascist theory. Rather, he was bothered by the fact that people could blind themselves to the threat of the Fascist state. It would never happen in Russia: "The reason [the members of the middle class] are hopeless, I think" he wrote in the thirties, "is because they have enough graft or, as they say, private incomes, to be lax and, as I say, corrupt. I don't know much about the workers, except that they haven't any of the 'properties, privileges and possessions' that have weakened the upper classes. They 'have nothing to lose but their chains.' "[12]

"The Fables"

Among the things that illustrate Steffens's drawing himself back from reporting and applying himself to the aesthetic and philosophic underpinnings of social change are a number of short anecdotes to which he gave the general title "the Fables," which were written between the early twenties and the thirties. By stating his ideas in parable or fable form, he was able to illustrate the soundness of his social concepts without directly referring to political reality or phrasing. Each "Fable" had one telling point, and, like most fables, was highly moralistic, direct, and instructive. Despite all attempts to make them look otherwise, however, they are essentially political. They have absolutely no subtlety. They present oversimplistic views of good versus evil, right versus wrong, liberalism versus conservatism, and action and progress versus indecision and stagnation.

Most often the villain of each fable, in one way or another, is a force resisting change and aiding the extension of the status quo. Often Steffens merely recounted some event that had illustrated to him a particular truth, making no attempt to present the incident as fiction. "Atlas: A Fable," referred to earlier, is an example, consisting only of Steffens's giving a biographical incident. Other examples are careful constructions built to emphasize a preconceived lesson. "The Light that Failed," for example, narrates how armies of red and white corpuscles were duped by parasites into working for the good of the parasites rather than for themselves and the man they supported. Misled by traitors from their own midst, the reds "became less and less red, more and more submissive, pink-white. . . . The whitest of the white corpuscles could see just ahead of them a time of prosperity, . . . but all of a sudden, the man died for lack of red corpuscles. . . ." Using the transparent microcosm of the man as the world, he had illustrated how greed—for money and luxury—had corrupted the desire for democracy, be it by reds or whites, and the obvious moral: "The classic experiment could not be carried on to a satisfactory conclusion—again."[13]

Among "the Fables" there are several pieces based upon supposed conversations with Satan. The tactic is a logical and useful device that Steffens had been rehearsing for years —shifting blame to so-called good men from so-called bad men, and reversing traditional definitions to force the reader to redefine his own beliefs. To employ this literary trick, he had to portray the devil as a tolerably likable fellow with human motives; the reader had to watch himself or he would become the devil's advocate out of self-defense.

The problem Steffens confronted in the Satan fables is, essentially, the same one he had pondered in his student days: he was trying to find a foundation for ethics. Muckraking had shown him the futility of seeking one among the "good" ele-

ments in society, and so, with his bearings shifted, he tried to
find out if the philosophical basis of the "bad" elements of society operated from any fundamental ethical convictions. Satan,
like Moses in *Moses in Red,* is viewed in sociological terms, his
standards based on functional consequences rather than on
abstract religion. Steffens had, at one time, intended to write a
piece about the length of *Moses in Red* using Satan as the central figure, but never completed anything that long.[14] He did,
however, brood considerably on the implications involved and
the insights he hoped he would inspire. The "good" people
would praise his Satan, he felt. He wrote to his friend Marie
Howe, wife of an old Ohio reformer, that his Satan stands for
"morality, reason, the maintenance of the species; and resists,
as evil, all progress, change, variation from the species." Since
he would thus represent the stalwarts of traditional social virtues, Steffens continued, it would be easy to see "why so many
of us found that we could be comfortable with bosses and
other honest crooks and loathed the righteous."[15]

Life in the Garden of Eden before man tasted the forbid-
den fruit was, as Satan described it to Steffens, " 'living like a
child in the nursery, busily, happily, without a thought of me
[Satan] and mine. I was nowhere. . . . No work was done except for fun or for mere beauty's sake. There was no sense of
use or duty; no law or order, none but God's. It was a waste.
It was pretty, perhaps, but I tell you, it wasn't decent. It was
not respectable.' "[16] Decency and respectability were not, in
Steffens's eyes, part of God's creation; they were, rather, innovations of the devil made for man to use in trying to de-
ceive both God and his fellow men. Morality and its enforcing
agent, conscience, were Satan's strongest weapons. With them
he could force people to follow his, not their own, desires.

Obviously the conscience was a collection of those social inhibitions that were taught in youth. Just as obviously, his new
son was a major factor in Steffens's turning his attention back
to basic sociological-philosophical-ethical problems in the abstract. He wanted none of the restrictions of traditional, sinful
morality and conscience burdening young Pete. His was to be

a world made better by his father's understanding; he would be taught new, realistic virtues. For him morality was to be replaced by naturalness, conscience by honesty, and respectability by happiness.

CHAPTER 8

Father

Pete

C LEARLY the most important reason for the shift in
Steffens's life-style came on November 21, 1924, with the
birth of his new son, Pete Stanley Steffens. To the fifty-eight-
year-old Steffens young Pete was a whole new world. In his
son Steffens saw the value of all he had learned, not as a collection of rules that he could teach his son, but as an illustration of one rule: that life had to be based on reality rather
than on the outdated and unworkable rules of the past. "I
teach my child," he wrote,

and, as I get the chance, I tell all the other children of all ages—pre-
school, in school, in college, and out:
   That nothing is done, finally and right.
   That nothing is known, positively and completely.
   That the world is theirs, all of it. It is full of jobs for them, full of
all sorts of things for them to find out and do, or do over and do
right. And they eat up the good news. They are glad, as I am, that
there is something left for them to discover and say and think and
do. Something? There is *everything* for youth to take over, and it is an
inspiration to them when I confess for all grown ups:
   That we have not now and never have had in the history of the
world a good government.
   That there is not now and never has been a perfectly run railroad,
school, newspaper, bank, theater, steel mill, factory, grocery store;
that no business is or ever has been built, managed, financed, as it
should be, must be and will be, some day—possibly in their day.[1]

Approaching child rearing with success, security, and experience behind him, Steffens could focus all his attention on
his son. And as is the case in such situations, his son was to

give in return a new vitality and youthful vision to his father that brightened and enlightened his writing with fresh and deceptively simple insights. Although he wrote humorously about the phenomenon of a man his age raising a son, there was more than a grain of truth in his query, "What self-respecting young father would encourage the mother of his child to avoid the menial tasks of the cradle in order himself to perform them and so work himself into and his wife out of the child. . . . I have discovered that for ages women have been elbowing us men out of the greatest happiness of life."[2]

Young Pete helped his father by giving him a new set of eyes. By imagining the world as his son saw it—as facts and realities devoid of axioms based on precedents—Steffens gained a new light on some of the foibles that had ensnared him on his journey through life.

By writing letters to Pete's maternal grandmother, as he assumed his son would if he knew how to write, Steffens explained the worth and purpose of the happenings that Pete observed as he grew. By so doing Steffens was stripping away years of ingrown beliefs, and the effect was much the same as taking the blinders off a horse. The new world he saw excited him; he had the experiences of a lifetime to add depth to his new youthful view.

In writing about his son, Steffens crystallized his ideas about the nature of society. "Children, like primitive man, like the animals, birds, and fishes," he wrote, "know not shame, and they don't need it. . . . Courtesy serves the whole purpose. . . . [Pete] does not understand shame but he knows it (or something) exists and he is quite willing to go around it—his way."[3] Through his son, Steffens could try to evaluate the effect of shame. But it was more than just shame; any aspect of behavior that was taught rather than innate was a fair target. In another place in the same essay he wrote, "I never tell him that I am right and that he is wrong," referring to his son. "We keep off the question of good and evil; we think more of strength and weakness, and it seems to me he 'gets' the difference and likes it."

The existence of various social levels—a foundation of the capitalistic system—was another fault that Steffens attacked via his son's education. "The theory I am working out," he informed readers of the *American,* "is that if a child can acquire a superiority complex before he is old enough to be a prig, he will achieve self-confidence and save his (inborn?) belief that he is 'as good as anybody'. . . . I let Pete win most of our battles; it hurts my pride, but it builds up his. I use my authority only when his safety is at stake and then I tell him that I conquer only because I am stronger than he is."[4]

Although he never coherently organized his opinions on education, after Pete's birth Steffens produced a steady stream of potshots at traditional methodology. Recalling his own education, he complained that he could not allow his own son to be subjected to such a society-centered system; education was intended to expand the individual, not extend the status quo. Before Pete's third birthday Steffens had reserved him a place in an experimental school being run by Bertrand Russell. "His idea," Steffens wrote to his brother-in-law, "is not to teach the kids any bunk, not to give them old physics, mathematics and economics, but from the start to teach them new knowledge."[5] Unfortunately, the family moved to the United States (and Russell's school failed) before Pete reached school age.

Steffens's preoccupation with education lasted the rest of his life. In fact, Pete's birth merely caused him to increase an interest that had existed for quite a few years already.

The Autobiography

By far the best evidence of his renewed concern in life as the result of fatherhood was the writing of his *Autobiography,* which he began in 1925. Pete was only one year old, and many of the reasons behind Steffens's wanting to write his life story are told in that fact. Indeed, the original title for the work was *A Life of Unlearning.* "I wanted to call it *A Life of Unlearning,*" he told his wife, "to show how I gained my picture of the world, how firmly They plant it in your mind so that it becomes almost impossible to change it."[6]

Once begun, the *Autobiography* became a task and, in another way, an obsession. He was recounting his life through the eyes of a father, and thus his story gained additional meaning. "The two preoccupations [the book and his son] seemed often to merge into one," his wife stated later. "As Steffens watched his son's progress, his thoughts went vividly back to his own childhood, and the first chapters of the *Life* readily took shape."[7] When one considers the number of things Steffens did in his life, it is surprising how large a portion of the work is devoted to his childhood. When young Pete is thought of as the audience, the way Steffens structured and told his story seems perfectly clear.

The *Autobiography* was not finished until 1930, after Steffens had moved back to America. The work itself is divided into five major sections; volume one consists of two sections: "A Boy On Horseback," which is twenty-three chapters long and recounts his life through his final year of college; and "Seeing New York First," which is an account of his introduction to the world of journalism. Volume two has three sections: "Muckraking," which covers his experience from the time he moved to *McClure's* through his work in attempting to reform Boston; "Revolution," which brings him through his marriage and child; and "Seeing America At Last," which brings him through 1930, and obviously was not conceived until he was well into writing the book.

In the beginning of the work Steffens rambles, painting a peaceful and interesting picture of a California childhood. His style is casual and, as one literary historian has noted, "the strange thing about his account is that at least at the beginning of his work he was certainly not aware of the enormous consequences it would have."[8] As the story progresses, the reader soon realizes that he is caught up in an increasingly complex, moving, and important work. The recounting of events alone is enough to make the *Autobiography* a standard reference on everything from the Progressive movement to the 1929 crash;

but beyond that is a personal story of compelling depth. "How he did study himself," Carl Sandburg later wrote of Steffens, "how he did try to fathom mankind by searching and cross-examining and spying on and carrying out counterespionage on the single specimen piece of humanity nearest and most available, the solitary and brooding Lincoln Steffens himself."[9]

Like other great autobiographies—Henry Adams's *Education* and Benjamin Franklin's *Autobiography* being good examples—Steffens's story of his own life should be taken with a grain of salt, and should be carefully compared to other records. It is a work written by a highly opinionated man whose insights and flashes of wisdom are carefully timed and planned to prove certain points of view. The lessons he extracted from the Progressive period, for example, would have been markedly different had Steffens himself not lost faith in capitalism. Written history, after all, requires a careful selection and skillful retelling of past events, and the perspective of a man writing his own history—with his own purposes in mind—does not lead to objectivity.

In fact, the weakness of self-analysis is as well illustrated by Steffens as is the strength. The significance of Steffens's role in the Mexican Revolution, for example, is quite exaggerated in his own account of the affair. While they are useful, and not incorrect, the portraits he draws of Wilson, Theodore Roosevelt, and numerous city and state bosses, and of Mussolini, to mention a few, are not nearly as complex or multidimensional as might be hoped. One entire love affair was omitted, albeit at the woman's request and against Steffens's wishes. All too often Steffens tells of events in which he has the last word. But the fact that his *Letters* were brought out soon after his death goes a long way toward correcting many weaknesses of the *Autobiography*.

In his own account of it, Steffens's life seems to be one cohesive unit, with every event a lesson leading inexorably to the next. The book gives the reader a carefully guided tour through sixty of America's most complex and interesting years in such a way that he never gets the feeling of being lost or perplexed. As the review for the *Nation* expressed it: "One reads it with a sense of getting one's bearings in a half-familiar territory for the first time: unrelated by-paths and gullies and hillocks gradually arrange themselves in an intelligible pattern, north becomes unmistakably north, and south south. One stands in a somewhat clearer relation than ever before to one's immediate predecessors. . . ."[10] The reader is able to associate himself with the subject to a remarkable degree, since Steffens had so many doubts common in the twentieth century. The *Autobiography* gives the reader a suprisingly new view of society, a view in which his life has clear meaning.

While such a response is obviously rewarding, there is also something unsettling about such a phenomenon. Any realistic historian finds everything too neat, too tidy a bundle. While the achievement of such an effect is a tribute to Steffens's writing ability, it is also usually a sign of some sort of oversimplication. One begins to suspect Steffens of falling victim to the same weakness of which he accused his fellow muckraker Charles Edward Russell: namely, that he "began with a solution and he proceeds from solution to solution. Not from problem to problem, you understand; he was no modern scientific researcher; he did not pass from question to question but from answer to answer."[11] Too often does one sense that some details must have been left out or tailored to fit Steffens's desired effect. Even the published form of his *Letters* is a mixed blessing, since it was edited by Steffens's wife and Granville Hicks, at that time a man of political leanings very similar to Steffens's.

Even considering these limitations, Steffens's *Autobiography* is a classic, ranking in the top half-dozen American autobiographies. Its greatest weakness as history—its biased point of view—is one of its greatest strengths as literature, for it always commands the attention and intellect of the reader. Steffens's forceful, humorous, driving, questioning personality enlivens the well-written narrative at every turn. Literary critic Heinrich Straumann placed the work in perspective, at least as a reformist document, when he wrote that "though judgement on the literary significance of the muckrakers has not yet been passed, it is quite possible that the autobiography of Lincoln Steffens will outlast most of the other literary productions concerned with the movement."[12] As an example of intellectual inquisitiveness, telling political and social insights, and fascinating historical documentation, one would have to go far to find an attempt more impressive.

The work, when published on April 9, 1931, by Harcourt, Brace and Company, was an immediate success. Brought out in the darkest days of the depression, at $7.50 a copy, it had to go into a second printing within ten days. Reviews were almost unanimously favorable, partially because the work was large enough to have a number of interpretations and critics were able to select whatever section best suited the political leanings of the particular magazine they were reviewing for. Within a year after publication a one-volume edition was issued, and sales have continued ever since.

In a dinner thrown for Steffens soon after the publication, he was, in a sense, returned to the public eyes. Testimonials were given for him by Clarence Darrow, Herbert Bayard Swope, and Haywood Broun; in attendance were Bernard Baruch, Frederic Howe, and eighty others. Telegrams of congratulations were received from numerous friends and well-wishers and, suprisingly, from ex-President Coolidge. Never was a telegram so incongruous.

In a nation still bewildered by the events of 1929 and the ever-darkening aftermath, the old liberal took on the aura of a prophet. The impressive number of important liberals he had known, his insider's view of many of the major events of the previous thirty years, his eternal optimism (which was occasionally exaggerated in the *Autobiography*), his fresh interpretation of America, and the charming style of his narrative all contributed to Steffens's glamor, at least among readers with a liberal bent; and 1931 was a particularly glum year for conservatives.

"Lincoln Steffens is old and gray," *Time* reported, "but not full of sleep. And what he has to say is nobody's pipe-dream but a meaty, marrowy, seasoned report on an active life which many a reader will envy."[13] The *Nation* credited the author with having "a wonderful intellectual plasticity against a background of intellectual integrity, an exceptional union of social imagination with personal intuitiveness." The *Nation,* understandably, also praised Steffens's liberalism: "If to be a prophet is to have a true humility of mind and spirit, to grasp imaginatively the conflicts of one's time, to apprehend the relation between man and events, to be capable of disenchantment without bitterness or negation, then Lincoln Steffens has been something of a prophet, and this book has something of the saintliness of prophecy."[14]

Delighted by his new success, Steffens took advantage of his regained fame, touring the country, joining in debates, giving lectures, publicizing his views (especially among youth), and, in general, promoting liberalism. He was given opportunities to write—including suggestions to write a third volume for the *Autobiography* and biographies of Boston liberal Edward Filene, and Wisconsin's Robert La Follette—which he rejected, having been confined too long by the rigors of works of such lengthy proportions. But when he could get a short assignment, where the end was clearly in view, he happily wrote, producing several good book reviews.

Homecoming

Enthused by accounts of a new, youthful spirit in America, Steffens had returned to his homeland in 1927. He was hopeful, once again, that he might be able to help secure the release of J. B. McNamara and redeem himself, but that was futile.

America, however, was no longer futile; it excited him. "Instead of showing America to my wife," he wrote, "it was she who began showing it to me. . . . She carried on one wall of her mind the European picture, made in England, of the United States and its people. She saw what she saw with the suprise of sharp contrasts," and, as usual, a new point of view was all that Steffens needed to get excited.[15] Beyond that, things had actually changed. He had left America with disappointment over what he felt to be the failure of reform—for him a personal failure. Not since World War I had he been a long-time resident, and the "roaring twenties" aspect of the culture had, by 1927, considerably altered the society.

For one thing the hypocrisy he had so detested was gone, at least after the crash. "One can't sneer any more that Washington is the kept woman of Wall Street," he wrote. "They are man and wife, and that changes everything; it makes the old wrong right. It makes Washington a decent woman."[16] Before his self-exile Steffens had been disgusted by politicians claiming to represent the people rather than business. While he disagreed with Coolidge and Hoover, at least they were open in their support of business as the supreme good. It was easier and more pleasant, after all, to live with a system which openly admitted it was at odds with his point of view, rather than in a society that denied the difference in an attempt to avoid the argument.

Also, he noted that the nature of American business—at least in some instances—had undergone some healthy changes. Industry had progressed to such a degree that over-production, not scarcity, was the problem. Need for a market to sell the products of industry forced businessmen to realize the necessity of paying workers enough to change them into a sufficiently consuming market.

Capitalism was becoming outdated, or modernized, Steffens felt. Founded in a world that had more people than goods to support them, capitalism had to be drastically altered if it hoped to adapt to a world where affluence was the situation. Slowly but surely he saw a compromise with the Soviet's ideas; while business might not admit to its sympathy with the new system, Steffens saw enough evidence to convince him that compromise, not conflict, was probable. "The United States," he wrote, ". . . is, however unconsciously, moving with mighty momentum on a course which seems not unlikely to carry our managing, investing, ruling masters of industry, politics, and art—by our blind method of trial and error—in the opposite direction around the world to the very same meeting place" as the Russians were aiming for.[17] The two enemies, he decided, "were more alike, essentially and politically, than any other two countries that I had seen."[18]

Steffens praised a new brand of American businessman, best exemplified by Henry Ford. Freeing himself from the tenacious hold of the bankers, Ford had gone into business with an honest and honorable goal. "He had started out in the usual thoughtless standard way with partners and later stockholders to raise capital, and his partners, typically, were men whose interest was not in making cheap cars for universal use but in making money." Ford, seeing that such a tactic was wasteful and would cause a price spiral and lessen his market, "abolished his stockholders to remove an obstacle to progress."[19] The parasites Steffens had detested were thus eliminated.

Ford had reversed the logic of business. Thinking of the customer rather than his own quick wealth, he "did not fix his price by taking the cost of a car and adding his profit." He was more logical; "he set his price at what the common mass of men . . . could pay," knowing that his costs would go down if his volume increased.[20]

By making the life of the workers better—economically more democratic—capitalism was co-opting the inevitable revolution that would result from economic disparity. If all men could share the common wealth, the workers would have far more to lose than their chains; they would, in short, have a vested interest in the business they worked for. With the growing size of industry and organized labor, the point of conflict would be dulled.

Even the arts reflected a compromise with old enemies. The people and the artist were starting to work on the same level. "The old arts of the theater, literature, painting have got too far ahead of the crowds to be understood by them," he wrote, "but business is doing its blind best by what we call contemptuously commercial art to show the work of painters, for example, in all sorts of advertising." Business, the bulwark of "the System," was co-opting the sources of discontent inadvertently, almost in spite of itself. "The blindest, most characteristic art movement of our age of machinery is the movie and the talkie movie, a new art that can include all the other arts. And mass producers, who are business men and not reformers, philanthropists and (not conscious) prophets, run their arts for the consuming masses, who rush in crowds to see and support it." Although traditional critics complained because Hollywood "could not 'raise' the cinema any faster than 'the mob' could go in appreciation," Steffens thought he "was seeing something new and wonderful under the sun through their tears and rage: that this new machine mass art cannot rise to its obviously potential heights without lifting and being lifted by the human race."[21]

Even the depression was full of good hope. Who in the rich days of the twenties would have believed the weaknesses of capitalism. But, with the economy of the country as proof, Steffens felt sure that capitalism's shortcomings were obvious to everyone. It would make people think. If telling people about socialism would not convince them before, it certainly would get a better chance now that they were hungry. The irony of poverty in the midst of plenty was too much to be overlooked.

EPILOGUE

A Measure of the Man

L INCOLN Steffens was a small, stocky fellow. His eyes were steel-blue and darted restlessly about from behind gold wire-rimmed glasses. He had brown hair that lightened to a dark blond when he was in his fifties, and which he combed forward in a bang over his forehead. He grew a full beard and moustache in his college days, soon after trimming down to a goatee and moustache, which he wore the rest of his life.

His lined, expressive face revealed a strong personality. He had, a female acquaintance noted, "a way of flashing up the corners of his mouth" that gave him a "sudden, lovely smile."[1] He sat, or stood, in that particular way which appears both totally at ease and yet keyed to immediate action. One cannot help comparing him to a cat, languid and casual, but agile and quick. His wife described his glance as "something devilish—or was it impish?"[2]

Descriptions of his personality are usually salted heavily with strong words: modifiers like mercurial, sophisticated, witty, ironic, thirsty, evasive, observant; nouns like artist, Socratic, skeptic, psychologist, avid searcher for truth, litterateur, and poseur. He drew strong reactions, whether negative or positive.

To those who disagreed with him he appeared cocky and conceited. They were, no doubt, correct to a certain degree. There was something about him, an air of self-assurance, an independence of spirit and intellect, that threatened the security of those who held views they had not examined well. His wife, when she first met him, compalined that he had a "bantering" tone and a "maddening, mellifluous voice" that sharpened her awareness of her own uncertainties. Mark Sullivan, a conservative journalist who worked briefly with Steffens at *McClure's* and who produced a whole shelf of shallow, overly nationalistic histories of the first decades of this century, seemed particularly upset by Steffens's penchant for ironies and liberalism:

> I felt that when one tried to hold him down to any orderly sequence of logical argument he took refuge in some evasive, grinning paradox. It was on one repartee of evasive paradox that some of his later fame rested—I tell the incident from memory: Asked by a finger-pointing inquisitor, "Are you a Communist?' he replied, "Oh, much worse—I'm a Christian. . . ."
>
> I was never free from feeling that he was in part a poseur —possibly a sincere poseur, that is, a poseur to himself. Once, during the Progressive Party convention at Chicago in 1912, Edward G. Lowry lunched with him. Afterwards Lowry said, "And there sat Steffens, talking revolution and blood—and sucking the guts out of a chocolate eclair impaled on an upright fork."[3]

"Iz" Durham, the boss of Philadelphia, once analyzed Steffens in the single line, " 'Oh, I can see that you are a born crook that's gone straight.' "[4] Because of that quality bosses and crooks trusted him, almost instinctively. He lacked that tone of moral censure, of righteous indignation, that made other reformers appear naïve or hypocritical. Other journalists could preach to the crooks, Steffens preached to the respectable.

In fact, Steffens had a habit of reversing situations, a talent for seeing the weakness in what others called strength and strength in what they called weakness. Instead of turning to them for support, Steffens blamed the reformers, the businessmen, and the churches for the corruption he fought. His fellow muckraker and friend Ray Stannard Baker recalled one particular example of what he called Steffens's "ironic counterpoises" when he wrote,

> I shall not forget a parable he made for me one day when we were out on an after-luncheon stroll:
> "Satan and I," said Steffens, "were walking down Fifth Avenue together when we saw a man stop suddenly and pick a piece of truth out of the air—right out of the air—a piece of living truth.

" 'Did you see that?' I asked Satan.

" 'Yes,' said Satan.

" 'Doesn't it worry you? Don't you know that it is enough to destroy you?'

" 'Yes, but I am not worried. I'll tell you why. It is a beautiful living thing now, but the man will first name it, then he will organize it, and by that time it will be dead. If he would let it live, and live it, it would destroy me. I'm not worried.' "[5]

Identifying Steffens as a muckraker, in fact, tends to distort his image into more of an accusor than a seeker. Reformer Frederic Howe, recalling his first impression of him, emphasizes this problem. Expecting a "militant reformer," he was surprised at the disparity between the image and the man: "The man who appeared had soft eyes and a quiet voice. Something unusual in the cut of his clothes, a pointed beard, and flowing tie suggested an artist."[6]

Indeed, reactions to Steffens often tell as much about the observer as the observed. To the open and robust newspaper publisher E. W. Scripps he was a "dapper little litterateur" who couldn't "help but be finicky; alike in ideas and in his person." To the emotional and sensitive Mable Dodge, on the other hand, "he was a delicately built little man, very flexible in his movements and with a rapier-keen mind." Ray Stannard Baker, to add a third witness, wrote that he "enjoyed the sudden, amusing, paradoxical quality of his mind."[7]

Until his son was born there was about Steffens an air of footloose independence best captured by a line from Jack Reed's poem to him: "Light-hearted liberty seems to belong to you."[8] Perhaps this freedom stems from his continual traveling or his inability to reach a decision that he knew he would always trust. Frederic Howe pointed out this changeableness when he wrote that "under the influence of Tom Johnson he came to believe in the single tax. Then he studied Socialism and became a Socialist without interest in Karl Marx, as he had been a single-taxer without adherence to Henry George. He hated sects and organization; organization, he said, would destroy the beauty of any movement."[9] But there was an element in his wandering that gave him strength. He wandered not aimlessly but always with a desire to find an intellectual home.

To some critics, especially the conservative ones, he ceased to be a searcher and became a propagandist when his radicalism became too strong. Ray Stannard Baker, for example, wrote:

I always thought he was at his best, doing his greatest work—in the sense of complete self-fulfillment—in the days when he was still the eager, observant, thirsty reporter striving first of all to understand. When the conscious reformer stepped in and took him over the less effective he seemed—to me—to be. I thought that he began to lose something of his objectivity, humility, even humor. He seemed no longer the avid searcher for truth: he knew what the truth was.[10]

There was a degree of truth in what Baker claimed. Steffens grew impatient when confronted by the philosophies he had himself dismissed. He and Baker had been working on the same level of liberalism; and when Steffens rejected that level and started to investigate another more radical one, Baker, and many others, viewed the change differently than Steffens did. Mark Sullivan, who changed levels in the opposite direction from Steffens, was almost vicious in reaction to Steffens's continued popularity. "His long tenure on fame was due," Sullivan reacted, "I think, to the fact that he was a radical, and, living on into a period in which much of the writing was done by radicals, he was more written about than some others who had similar claim to fame. To the younger generation of literary radicals who succeeded him, Steffens was the old master, and they celebrated him." (One cannot help observing that later in the same source Sullivan claims that he, not Steffens, had actually written the first muckraking article.)[11]

But, while Baker and Sullivan thought that Steffens had carried his liberalism too far and then hardened into a propagandist, other critics attest to his continued inquisitiveness. After Steffens's death historian and poet Carl Sandburg wrote of Steffens that "he never let up on these fishing expeditions into the deep sea currents, the sun spots and ice floes, of his swarming alive mind." Later Sandburg adds, "He had ways kin to Socrates, the asker of questions, whims allying him to Diogenes, who with mockery and a lantern sought an honest man by daylight in the streets of Athens—or to any newly arrived Irishman saying, 'Have you got a government here? Yes? Then I'm against it.' " And finally, he adds, "He had enough doubts and faiths to make a classic."[12]

The question of whether Steffens stopped being a student and became a propagandist will never be fully answered, of course, since it depends on the degree of liberalism of the observer. Steffens talked and wrote, and whatever he happened to believe worked its way into his talk and writing. Thus, his writing at any single point in time can be interpreted as propagandistic for some ideal; but he was an untrustworthy propagandist, for he was soon poking holes in his own past beliefs. The working title for his *Autobiography*, remember, was *A Life of Unlearning*. One cannot help but agree with his own statement about himself: "I am more curious about this darned world than I am certain about it."[13]

His greatest talent was as a journalist. He wrote clearly and effectively. His style became smoother as he grew older. He was always at his best recounting some experience that illustrated a point, be it with President Roosevelt or Lenin. He did not fare well when he ventured into the abstract or philosophical too deeply, and most of the time he sensed that fact. He usually broached the abstract in concrete terms, with examples from experience.

Although he occasionally attempted to write short stories, he was better at reporting. Most of the fiction he wrote was only lightly veiled experience, and in almost every case it consisted of the narrator of the story meeting a radical who would explain the source of his radicalism by relating past experience and convert the narrator, and hopefully the reader, to his way of thinking. The closest he came to being successful in fiction was in "the Fables," which were, after all, experiences with lessons that could be handled like news events. His one major attempt at philosophy, *Moses In Red*, was a mistake.

Always at ease, well mannered, witty, and charming, he dis-

armed the most reticent public figures by his sincere interest
in the story he was after. Thus, men like New York's Boss
Croker—whom he always called Mr. Richard Croker—and
Philadelphia's "Iz" Durham, men who were used to being
roughly treated by the press and who had good reason to fear
Steffens as a journalist, often told him much more than they
would tell anyone else. Steffens was easy to talk to. He listened
well, and let the speaker ramble on as he saw fit to ramble.
Such men appreciated the fact that, unlike the rest of the reporters they met, Steffens did not morally condemn them;
they realized that he had a genuine interest, and so they
talked—often off the record, but they talked. With Steffens
they were gentlemen, and they appreciated the feeling. And
since Steffens was a gentleman, he appreciated their position
and, when he said he would, he respected their confidences.
W. A. Swanberg, the biographer of William Randolph Hearst,
complimented Steffens's ability as an interviewer, writing that
he "accomplished a miracle" when he successfully interviewed
Hearst, a feat no other reporter ever accomplished. Hearst
himself went so far as to say that Steffens "was the best interviewer he had ever encountered."[14]

But Steffens, like his readers, formed his own opinions, and
he included those opinions in his writing. He was not content
merely to report, he also analyzed. Realizing that any reporting entailed judgment, he never attempted to veil his opinions. Since he did not condemn the "bosses" or the "Communists," as other writers did, he received a fair share of criticism. Mark Sullivan, for example, wrote:

He was called a great reporter. In his younger, obscure newspaper
days he may have been, but in his better-known writing I rarely saw a
paragraph that I would have called great reporting. Hardly would I
have called it reporting at all. . . . [He was] not objective at all, but at
once psychic and subjective. He probed into, or surmised, the inner
mind and motives of a mayor or boss; then he wrote what Lincoln
Steffens thinks about what Lincoln Steffens conceives to be the mind
of the mayor of Minneapolis, or Philadelphia, or whatever.[15]

Writing came hard to Steffens. He had the habit of perfecting each paragraph before continuing, and would often re-work a single line dozens of times before he was satisfied. It took him weeks to complete a single article.

His *Autobiography*, by far the longest and best of all his writing, was actually begun by his wife, who secretly copied several of his anecdotes as he told them and, when she had about fifty pages, showed them to him. He got the idea, but he still bogged down often. His wife began stealing a completed section of the manuscript and sending it to the typist; he would be satisfied when he saw it in type. Later she took to sending sections to a friend of Steffens's who would read them and send encouraging letters urging him to continue. It was probably because he was writing for his son and friends that his *Autobiography*, like his letters, is far more readable than his artilces were.[16]

His writing showed the greatest quality in terms of clarity. Steffens was not an artist with words; rather, he was a social thinker. He had a limited but certain writing ability which he employed to achieve an end; it was the end and not the medium that he was best at. As long as his writing accomplished thought he was successful.

He had little tricks of style that he used often, which make his writing fairly easy to identify. He used the dash, for example, time and again in efforts to add ironic twists by reversing what the reader expected, as in the statement "Because if the honest voter cared no more for his party than the politician, then the honest vote would govern, and that would be bad—for graft," or "I trust the reformers will pick up some 'pointers' from—Chicago."[17]

He was a dreadful speller and had penmanship that would make a pharmacist shudder. One of the reasons for his poor penmanship may have been a desire to hide his spelling. However, his manuscripts were typed throughout his career by Miss R. M. Ford, who accomplished something of a miracle.

Steffens enjoyed lecturing, which came to him naturally. He was an effective orator, and at the various high points in his career was sought by all sorts of liberal causes. He participated in numerous debates on subjects ranging from "the System" to woman's suffrage. His reputation as a radical was probably as much due to his speaking as to his writing, especially in the first years of the century when his articles were edited and often printed in watered-down form. In a letter to his brother-in-law he wrote that "a speech is a combination of the forces of the speaker and the audience.... [My speech] is usually a narrative, founded on chronology. But as I look over an audience, I get their status, mood, etc.... I extend a statement to clear off a frown, I shorten a statement when I see they have got it. I feel my way."[18] He rarely used notes, as they were more of a hindrance than a help. In particular he enjoyed speaking to young people who had not yet learned what they were supposed to—according to "the System"—reject, and who were consequently interested and trusting.

Since a man's place in history is determined by his accomplishments, Steffens will be most remembered as a muckraker rather than a revolutionary or a radical. It was in that role that he was preeminent, and it was by his writing during his muckraking years that he accomplished the most. His other accomplishments, while significant, would not have made him famous, and they did not have the impact or importance of muckraking on American history.

But it is his attitude, not his work, that makes the story of his life important yet today. There were other muckrakers who accomplished almost as much, who were more talented as writers, who are all but forgotten today. What they lacked, and what Steffens had, was a mode of thinking, of constant inquisitiveness, of innate liberalism that made his life an example of continual self-education.

Once, after Steffens had given a lecture, a couple of old ladies told his wife, "We've found out what he is! He's a Christian Science Utopian Socialist Democrat!"[19] While they may have come close, they had not quite pinpointed his leanings—but then, neither has anyone else.

For it was his constant belief that by seeking, by questioning, by refusing to give in to habit, he could help, however minutely, in making a better world.

A few years before they were married, he wrote to Ella Winter, "Up to now I am an awfully doubting listener to all theories; theories, I say; and there is nothing else in so called human knowledge except theories. Is there?"[20] Constantly doubting everything, he was still an optimist, for by doubting he became his own man, sometimes wrong and often disliked, but always free and always an individual. He never stopped learning, and he never stopped growing.

When he was in college Steffens discovered a problem: "that it was philosophically true, in a most literal sense, that nothing is known; that it is precisely the foundation that is lacking for science; that all we call knowledge rest[s] upon assumptions which the scientists [do] not accept."[21] He spent his life searching for that foundation, and when he found something he thought might end his search, he tested it and retested it, hoping for success, finding weakness, A twentieth-century Don Quixote, his hopeful journey never ended. "This little Machiavellian, itinerant preacher went up and down upon the earth shaking it in his own way," Mabel Dodge recalled. "He said the same things over and over, gently, subtly, and unendingly. As one note, sounded on a violin string in just the right vibration and in sufficient volume, may shatter solid material and bring down a house in ruins, Steff's delicate music undoubtedly had its share in collapsing the civilization of the twentieth century."[22]

Steffens ended his own story with this thought:

I have not lived in vain. The world which I tried so hard, so dumbly, to change has changed me. . . . My life was worth my living. And as for the world in general, all that was or is or ever will be wrong with that is my—our thinking about it.[23]

How many men who have doubted or questioned the world as much as Steffens can make as hopeful and affirmative a statement as this: "My life was worth my living."

Notes and References

Chapter 1

1. Lincoln Steffens, *The Autobiography of Lincoln Steffens*, 2 vols. (New York: Harcourt, Brace and Co., 1931), I, p. 310.
2. *Ibid.*, II, p. 358.
3. Steffens, *The Letters of Lincoln Steffens*, ed. by Ella Winter and Granville Hicks, with memorandum by Carl Sandburg, 2 vols. (New York: Harcourt, Brace and Co., 1938), I, p. 202.
4. Steffens, *Autobiography*, II, p. 606.
5. *Ibid.*, p. 608.
6. *Ibid.*, p. 705.
7. *Ibid.*, p. 712.
8. Steffens, *Letters*, I, pp. 398–99.
9. Steffens, *The World of Lincoln Steffens*, ed. by Ella Winter and Herbert Shapiro (New York: Hill and Wang, 1962), p. 47.
10. *Ibid.*, p. 54.
11. Steffens, *Autobiography*, I, p. 161.
12. Mabel Dodge Luhan, *Movers and Shakers*, vol. 3 of *Intimate Memories* (New York: Harcourt, Brace and Co., 1936), p. 68.
13. Steffens, *Letters*, II, p. 908.
14. Steffens, *Lincoln Steffens Speaking* (New York: Harcourt, Brace and Company, 1936), p. ix.
15. Ella Winter, *And Not To Yield: An Autobiography* (New York: Harcourt, Brace & World, Inc., 1963), p. 214.
16. *Ibid.*, pp. 214–15.

Chapter 2

1. Steffens, *Autobiography*, I, p. 25.
2. *Ibid.*, p. 47.
3. *Ibid.*, pp. 114–15.
4. *Ibid.*, p. 119.
5. *Ibid.*, p. 127.
6. Steffens, *Letters*, I, p. 27.
7. *Ibid.*, I, p. 12.
8. Steffens, *Autobiography*, I, p. 140.
9. Steffens, *Letters*, I. pp. 18–19.
10. *Ibid.*, p. 39.
11. *Ibid.*, p. 54.

12. *Ibid.*, p. 73.

13. Otis L. Graham, Jr., *The Great Campaigns: Reform and War in America, 1900–1928*, History of the American People Series (Englewood Cliffs, N.J.: Prentice-Hall, Inc., 1971), p. 127.

14. Arthur M. Schlesinger, Jr., *The Crisis of the Old Order*, vol. 1 of *The Age of Roosevelt* (Boston: Houghton Mifflin Company, 1957), p. 208.

Chapter 3

1. Richard Hofstadter, *The Age of Reform* (New York: Vintage Books, 1955), p. 188.

2. *Ibid.*, p. 186.

3. Steffens, *Letters*, I, pp. 93–94.

4. *Ibid.*, p. 98.

5. Steffens, *Autobiography*, I, p. 231.

6. Norman Hapgood, *The Changing Years: Reminiscences of Norman Hapgood* (New York: Farrar & Reinhart, 1930), pp. 107–08.

7. Steffens, *Autobiography*, I, p. 237.

8. *Ibid.*, p. 220.

9. *Ibid.*, p. 274.

10. *Ibid.*, II, p. 417.

11. Steffens, *Letters*, I, p. 108.

12. Steffens, *Autobiography*, I, p. 258.

13. Steffens, *Letters*, I, p. 82.

14. Steffens, *Autobiography*, I, p. 315.

15. Hutchins Hapgood, *A Victorian in the Modern World* (New York: Harcourt, Brace and Company, 1939), pp. 138–39.

16. William Allan White, *The Autobiography of William Allan White* (New York: Macmillan Company, 1946), p. 301.

17. Steffens, *Autobiography*, II, p. 363.

18. Ray Stannard Baker, *American Chronicle: The Autobiography of Ray Stannard Baker* (New York: Charles Scribner's Sons, 1945), p. 96.

19. S. S. McClure, *My Autobiography* (New York: Fred A. Stokes, 1915), p. 245.

20. Baker, pp. 201–04.

21. Steffens, *Autobiography*, II. p. 581.

Chapter 4

1. Steffens, *The Shame of the Cities* (1904; rpt. New York: Sagamore Press, Inc., 1957), pp. 22–23.

2. Louis Filler, *The Muckrakers: Crusaders for American Liberalism* (Chicago: Henry Regnery Co., 1968), p. 96.

3. Steffens, *Autobiography*, II, p. 376.

4. *Ibid.,* p. 329.
5. Steffens, *Shame of the Cities,* pp. 10–11.
6. *Ibid.,* p. 11.
7. Steffens, *Autobiography,* II, p. 443.
8. Steffens, *Letters,* I, p. 172.
9. Steffens, *Shame of the Cities,* p. 20.
10. Steffens, *Autobiography,* II, p. 492.
11. Steffens, *The Struggle for Self-Government* (1906; rpt. New York: Johnson Reprint Corp., 1968), p. 42.
12. Russel B. Nye, *Progressive Midwestern Politics* (East Lansing: Michigan State University Press, 1959), p. 114.
13. Steffens, "It," *Everybody's Magazine,* September 1910, 292.
14. *Ibid.,* November 1910, 648.
15. *Ibid.,* December 1910, 873.
16. Steffens, *Autobiography,* II, pp. 408–09.
17. Filler, p. 99.
18. Steffens, *Autobiography,* II, p. 596.
19. *Ibid.,* p. 409.
20. Steffens, *Shame of the Cities,* pp. 7,8.
21. Steffens, "It," December 1910, 825.
22. Steffens, *Struggle for Self-Government,* pp. vi–vii.
23. Steffens, *Shame of the Cities,* p. 6.
24. Richard Hofstadter, *The Age of Reform,* p. 205.
25. Steffens, "National Bankers Graft," *St. Louis Post-Dispatch,* March 25, 1906, Section 3, p. 4.
26. Lloyd Morris, *Postscript to Yesterday* (New York: Random House, 1947), p. 289.
27. Steffens, *Autobiography,* II, p. 632.
28. *Ibid.,* p. 375.
29. Steffens, *Letters,* I, p. 207.
30. *Ibid.,* pp. 197, 199.
31. Steffens, *Autobiography,* II, pp. 492–93.
32. *Ibid.,* pp. 417–18.
33. Steffens, *Letters,* I, p. 185.
34. *Ibid.,* pp. 204, 208.
35. *Ibid.,* p. 203.
36. David M. Chalmers, *The Social and Political Ideas of the Muckrakers* (New York: Citadel Press, 1964), p. 80.
37. Steffens, *Autobiography,* II, p. 409.
38. *Ibid.,* p. 493.
39. Frederic C. Howe, *The Confessions of a Reformer* (1925; rpt. Chicago: Quadrangle Books, 1967), p. 182.
40. Steffens, *Autobiography,* II, p. 411.
41. Steffens, *Struggle for Self-Government,* p. 133.
42. Belle Case and Floa La Follette, *Robert M. La Follette: June 14,*

1885–June 18, 1925, 2 vols. (New York: Macmillan, 1953), I, 182.

43. Robert S. Maxwell, *La Follette and the Rise of Progressivism in Wisconsin* (n.p.: State Historical Society of Wisconsin, 1956), p. 71.

44. Peter Lyon, *Success Story: The Life and Times of S. S. McClure* (New York: Charles Scribners' Sons, 1963), pp. 220–22; 224–28.

45. Henry F. May, *The End of Innocence* (Chicago, Quadrangle Books, 1959), p. 183.

46. Steffens, *Autobiography,* II, p. 614.

47. *Ibid.,* p. 618.

48. *Ibid.,* p. 616.

49. *Ibid.,* p. 606.

Chapter 5

1. Steffens, *Autobiography,* II, p. 661.
2. Steffens, *Letters,* I, p. 280.
3. Steffens, *Autobiography,* II, pp. 677–78.
4. *Ibid.,* p. 688.
5. Mabel Dodge Luhan, *Movers and Shakers,* p. 67.
6. Steffens, *Letters,* I, p. 281.
7. Ella Winter, *And Not to Yield,* pp. 123–24.
8. Hutchins Hapgood, *A Victorian in the Modern World,* p. 348.
9. Luhan, p. 80.
10. *Ibid.,* p. 83.
11. *Ibid.,* p. 172.
12. Steffens, *The World of Lincoln Steffens,* p. 236.
13. Steffens, *Autobiography,* II, p. 655.
14. Steffens, *Letters,* I, p. 347.

Chapter 6

1. Steffens, *The World of Lincoln Steffens,* p. 23.
2. Steffens, *Letters,* I, p. 366.
3. Steffens, "Into Mexico and — Out," *Everybody's Magazine,* May 1916, p. 563.
4. Steffens, *The World of Lincoln Steffens,* p. 4.
5. Steffens, *Autobiography,* II, pp. 729–31.
6. Steffens, *Letters,* I, p. 363.
7. Steffens, *Autobiography,* II, p. 729.
8. Steffens, "Into Mexico and — Out," pp. 537, 540.
9. Steffens, *Letters,* I, pp. 369–70.
10. *Ibid.,* p. 377; Steffens, *Autobiography,* II, p. 739.
11. Steffens, *Letters,* I, p. 383.
12. *Ibid.,* p. 351.
13. Steffens, *Autobiography,* II, p. 717.

14. Steffens, *The World of Lincoln Steffens,* p. 24.
15. Steffens, *Autobiography,* II, p. 725.
16. Steffens, *Letters,* I, p. 378.
17. Steffens, *Autobiography,* II, p. 718.
18. *Ibid.,* pp. 720–21.
19. *Ibid.,* p. 757.
20. Steffens, *Letters,* I, pp. 399–400.
21. Steffens, *Autobiography,* II, p. 758.
22. Steffens, *World of Lincoln Steffens,* p. 41.
23. *Ibid.,* p. 44.
24. *Ibid.,* p. 42.
25. Steffens, *Letters,* I, p. 406.
26. *Ibid.,* p. 407.
27. *Ibid.,* p. 463.
28. *Ibid.,* pp. 468–69.
29. Steffens, *World of Lincoln Steffens,* p. 63.
30. *Ibid.,* p. 59.
31. *Ibid.*
32. *Ibid.,* p. 56.
33. *Ibid.,* p. 59.
34. Steffens, *Autobiography,* II, p. 798.
35. Steffens, *Lincoln Steffens Speaking,* p. 64.
36. N. Gordon Levin, Jr., *Woodrow Wilson and World Politics* (New York: Oxford University Press, 1968), p. 213.
37. Arthur Walworth, *Woodrow Wilson,* 2nd rev. ed. (Baltimore: Penguin Books, 1965), p. 291n.
38. Steffens, *World of Lincoln Steffens,* p. 75.
39. *Ibid.,* p. 91.
40. *Ibid.,* p. 83.
41. Steffens, *Letters,* II, p. 545.
42. Steffens, *World of Lincoln Steffens,* p. 87.
43. *Ibid.,* p. 89.
44. *Ibid.,* p. 90.
45. *Ibid.,* p. 101.

Chapter 7

1. Steffens, *Letters,* II, p. 651.
2. Steffens, *World of Lincoln Steffens,* p. 162.
3. Steffens, *Letters,* II, p. 629.
4. *Ibid.,* p. 651.
5. Mabel Dodge Luhan, *Movers and Shakers,* p. 67.
6. Steffens, *Letters,* I, p. 492.
7. Ella Winter, *And Not to Yield,* pp. 103–04.

8. Carlos Baker, *Ernest Hemingway: A Life Story* (New York: Bantam Books, 1969), p. 134.
9. Steffens, *Autobiography*, II, pp. 815–16.
10. *Ibid.*, II, p. 817.
11. Steffens, *Lincoln Steffens Speaking*, pp. 240–41.
12. *Ibid.*, pp. 174–75.
13. Steffens, *World of Lincoln Steffens*, p. 159.
14. Steffens, *Letters*, II, p. 630.
15. *Ibid.*, p. 699.
16. Steffens, *World of Lincoln Steffens*, p. 189.

Chapter 8

1. Steffens, *Lincoln Steffens Speaking*, pp. 147–48; compare to Steffens, *Autobiography*, I, p. 126.
2. Steffens, *Lincoln Steffens Speaking*, pp. 39–40.
3. Steffens, *World of Lincoln Steffens*, p. 197.
4. *Ibid.*, p. 201.
5. Steffens, *Letters*, II, p. 781
6. Ella Winter, *And Not to Yield*, p. 111.
7. Steffens, *Letters*, II, p. 671.
8. Heinrich Straumann, *American Literature in the Twentieth Century*, 3rd rev. ed. (New York: Harper Torchbooks, 1965), p. 10.
9. Steffens, *Letters*, I, pp. vii–viii.
10. Newton Arvin, "Epitaph for a Generation," *Nation*, April 15, 1931, p. 415.
11. Steffens, *Lincoln Steffens Speaking*, pp. 157–58.
12. Straumann, p. 11.
13. *Time*, May 4, 1931, p. 63.
14. Arvin, p. 415.
15. Steffens, *Autobiography*, II, p. 849.
16. *Ibid.*, p. 863.
17. *Ibid.*, p. 872.
18. *Ibid.*, p. 851.
19. *Ibid.*, pp. 853–54.
20. *Ibid.*, pp. 852–53.
21. *Ibid.*, pp. 870-71.

Epilogue

1. Mabel Dodge Luhan, *Movers and Shakers*, p. 66.
2. Ella Winter, *And Not to Yield*, p. 53.
3. Mark Sullivan, *The Education of An American* (New York: Blue Ribbon Books, 1938), p. 200.

4. Steffens, *Autobiography*, II, p. 414.
5. Ray Stannard Baker, *American Chronicle*, p. 222.
6. Frederic C. Howe, *Confessions of a Reformer*, p. 182.
7. Negley D. Cochran, *E. W. Scripps* (New York: Harcourt, Brace and Co., 1933), p. 146; Luhan, *Movers and Shakers*, p. 66; Baker, *American Chronicle*, p. 122.
8. Luhan, p. 172.
9. Howe, p. 184.
10. Baker, p. 223.
11. Sullivan, p. 199.
12. Steffens, *Letters*, I, pp. viii–ix.
13. *Ibid.*, I, p. 458.
14. W. A. Swanberg, *Citizen Hearst* (New York: Bantam Books, 1961), pp. 492–95; Steffens, *Autobiography*, II, p. 541.
15. Sullivan, pp. 199–200.
16. Winter, pp. 111–13.
17. Steffens, *Shame of the Cities*, pp. 5, 163.
18. Steffens, *Letters*, II, pp. 574–75.
19. *Ibid.*, I, p. xvii.
20. *Ibid.*, II, p. 568.
21. Steffens, *Autobiography*, I, p. 127.
22. Luhan, p. 69.
23. Steffens, *Autobiography*, II, pp. 872–73.

Selected Bibliography

PRIMARY SOURCES

The Autobiography of Lincoln Steffens. 2 vols. New York: Harcourt, Brace and Company, 1931. It has all the disadvantages of any self-analysis, but is still the best place to begin any research on Steffens. More space is devoted to the earlier period of his life, with only one section out of five touching on the years after 1925, and that the briefest one. It ends, of course, in 1930.

The Letters of Lincoln Steffens. Ed. Ella Winter and Granville Hicks with memorandum by Carl Sandburg. 2 vols. New York: Harcourt, Brace and Company, 1938. Despite the fact that they were edited by Steffens's widow and a good friend, the *Letters* are remarkably balanced. They fill in much that the *Autobiography* leaves out, especially giving details about Steffens's daily routine and personal affairs. They emphasize the latter part of his life. Although it contains some errors in detail, there is an extremely useful list of most of Steffens's published works in the appendix.

The Shame of the Cities. 1904; rpt. New York: Sagamore Press, Inc., 1957. A collection of Steffens's early magazine articles about municipal corruption. Steffens's first book, and the best of his muckraking. This edition contains an excellent introduction by Louis Joughin.

Lincoln Steffens Speaking. New York: Harcourt, Brace and Company, 1936. The last book of Steffens's writings that he personally helped in compiling. It contains several previously published articles and sketches, plus a few previously unpublished comments. All the materials concern his work between the publication of the *Autobiography* in 1931 and his death. Of mostly very short pieces, it is good in giving the flavor of his character.

The Struggle for Self-Government. 1906; rpt. New York: Johnson Reprint Corp., 1968. Steffens's second volume of muckraking articles, this time concerned with corruption at the state level. This volume should be read after *The Shame of the Cities,* as it is a continuation of the same thesis. Of particular interest is Steffens's "Dedication to the Czar of Russia."

The Upbuilders. 1909; rpt. Seattle: University of Washington Press, 1969. The least important of the volumes of muckraking. It contains character sketches of various city- and state-level reformers.

The World of Lincoln Steffens. Ed. Ella Winter and Herbert Shapiro. New York: Hill and Wang, 1962. A collection of various articles from the post-muckraking years, compiled by Steffens's widow and a collaborator. It is useful because it brings together a good sampling of Steffens's writing. The particular selections illustrate the range of his ability and interests. It is also about the only available source of *Moses in Red.*

SECONDARY SOURCES

1. Biographies and Autobiographies

BAKER, RAY STANNARD. *American Chronicle: The Autobiography of Ray Stannard Baker.* New York: Charles Scribner's Sons, 1945. Contains some interesting observations on the men at *McClure's* The book itself is interesting and informative; it reminds one of Steffens's *Autobiography.*

HAPGOOD, HUTCHINS. *A Victorian in the Modern World.* New York: Harcourt, Brace and Company, 1939. Hutchins was the most radical of the Hapgood brothers, and for this reason his autobiography is the most interesting. Contains a good deal of material about Mable Dodge and the intellectuals in New York. Hapgood knew Steffens for most of his adult life and has many interesting stories about him. A good book.

HOWE, FREDERIC C. *The Confessions of a Reformer,* 1925; rpt. Chicago: Quadrangle Books, 1967. An interesting story well told. A good character sketch of Steffens as a muckraker.

LUHAN, MABEL DODGE. *Movers and Shakers.* Vol. 3 of *Intimate Memories.* New York: Harcourt, Brace and Company, 1936. A fascinating story of a fascinating woman. She knew Steffens well and draws one of the best character sketches of him during the teens of this century.

LYONS, PETER. *Success Story: The Life and Times of S. S. McClure.* New York: Scribners, 1963. The best biography of McClure and an excellent overview of the whole era. It contains considerable original research on almost everything concerned with McClure. It is far better than McClure's *My Autobiography.*

SULLIVAN, MARK. *The Education of an American.* New York: Blue Ribbon Books, 1938. Sullivan attacks Steffens every chance he gets. Worth reading if only to get the other side of the story. Sullivan illustrates what happened to many of the muckrakers.

WHITE, WILLIAM ALLEN. *The Autobiography of William Allan White*. New York: Macmillan, 1946. An interesting account of an average American's view of muckraking by a man who was only slightly involved. Well-written and useful history.

WINTER, ELLA. *And Not to Yield: An Autobiography*. New York: Harcourt, Brace and World, 1963. An essential source for information on Steffens's later years. A loving and informative portrait is painted by Steffens's widow in her own account.

2. Histories

CHALMERS, DAVID MARK. *The Social and Political Ideas of the Muckrakers*. New York: Citadel Press, 1964. A good account of the philosophies of most of the major muckrakers as far as it goes, but far too short to handle the subject.

FILLER, LOUIS. *The Muckrakers: Crusaders for American Liberalism*. Chicago: Henry Regnery Company, 1968. The standard work on the muckrakers. Filled with searching comments and original research, it is the starting point for anyone wishing to study the movement as a whole.

HOFSTADTER, RICHARD. *The Age of Reform: From Bryan to F.D.R.* New York: Vintage Press, 1955. Chapter five, "The Progressive Impulse," is a particularly good study of the reasoning behind what the muckrakers were doing. The whole book is a classic example of scholarship.

LEVIN, N. GORDON. *Woodrow Wilson and World Politics: America's Response to War and Revolution*. New York: Oxford University Press, 1968. Contains valuable material on the Bullitt Mission.

MAY, HENRY F. *The End of American Innocence: A Study of the First Years of Our Own Times, 1912–1917*. Chicago: Quadrangle Books, 1959. A fine study of the radicals in New York, including a particularly interesting characterization of Steffens.

REIGER, C. C. *The Era of the Muckrakers*. Chapel Hill, N.C.: University of North Carolina Press, 1936.

WALWORTH, ARTHUR. *Woodrow Wilson*. 2nd rev. ed. Baltimore, Md.: Penguin Books, 1965. Contains interesting accounts of Wilson's reaction to the Bullitt Mission.

WILSON, HAROLD S. *McClure's Magazine and the Muckrakers*. Princeton: Princeton University Press, 1970.

3. Essays and Articles

COCHRAN, BUD T. "Lincoln Steffens and the Art of Autobiography." *College Composition*, 14 (1963).

KAPLIN, JUSTIN. "He Searched for Truth and Glimpsed the Future."
    New York Times Book Review, August 31, 1969.
MADISON, CHARLES A. "Lincoln Steffens: Muckrakers Progress." In
    Critics & Crusaders: A Century of American Protest. New York:
    Holt, 1941.
MUMFORD, LOUIS. "The Shadow of the Muck-Rake." In *The Golden
    Day.* 1926; rpt. New York: Dover Publishers, 1953. An excellent
    essay illustrating the position of muckraking in the literature of
    the times.
ROLLINS, ALFRED B. "The Heart of Lincoln Steffens." *South Atlantic
    Quarterly,* 1960.

Index